MATTHEW HALL

NLP Secrets

Your Helpful Guide To Understand The Secrets And Techniques Of NLP And Persuasion To Become The Master Of Your Success

Copyright © 2020 Matthew Hall

All rights reserved.

© **Copyright 2020 - All rights reserved.**

The content contained within this book may not be reproduced, duplicated or transmitted without direct written permission from the author or the publisher.

Under no circumstances will any blame or legal responsibility be held against the publisher, or author, for any damages, reparation, or monetary loss due to the information contained within this book. Either directly or indirectly.

Legal Notice:

This book is copyright protected. This book is only for personal use. You cannot amend, distribute, sell, use, quote or paraphrase any part, or the content within this book, without the consent of the author or publisher.

Disclaimer Notice:

Please note the information contained within this document is for educational and entertainment purposes only. All effort has been executed to present accurate, up to date, and reliable, complete information. No warranties of any kind are declared or implied. Readers acknowledge that the author is not engaging in the rendering of legal, financial, medical or professional advice. The content within this book has been derived from various sources. Please consult a licensed professional before attempting any techniques outlined in this book.

By reading this document, the reader agrees that under no circumstances is the author responsible for any losses, direct or indirect, which are incurred as a result of the use of information contained within this document, including, but not limited to, — errors, omissions, or inaccuracies.

Table of Content

Introduction 5

Chapter 1. Neuro-Linguistic Programming (NLP) 10

Chapter 2. How NLP Works, Importance of NLP, and is NLP Effective? 17

Chapter 3. Components of NLP and NLP Techniques 23

Chapter 4. The Swish Pattern... 28

Chapter 5. Hypnosis... 35

Chapter 6. Brainwashing 41

Chapter 7. How to Use NLP for in Sales 46

Chapter 8. How to Use NLP in Relationships............................. 49

Chapter 9. NLP in Business 55

Chapter 10. Body Language and Behavior Imitation 62

Chapter 11. Using NLP to Manage People 68

Chapter 12. Protecting Yourself From NLP Mind Control 74

Chapter 13. Smart and Wise Goal-Setting Using Neuro-Linguistics 79

Chapter 14. Introduction of Persuasion 83

Chapter 15. History of Persuasion.. 87

Chapter 16. Six Principles of Persuasion..................................... 91

Chapter 17. Theories on Persuasion... 96

Chapter 18. Persuasion Techniques.. 99

Chapter 19. Difference Between Persuasion and Manipulation .. 106

Chapter 20. Factors That Influence Persuasion 110

Chapter 21. Methods of Persuasion and Tricks Used By Mass Media And Advertising 115

Chapter 22. The Benefits of Learning About Persuasion............. 118

Chapter 23. Dark Persuasion 124

Chapter 24. Covert Persuasion..129

Chapter 25. Ethical Persuasion..133

Chapter 26. Difference Between Persuasion and Negotiation.....139

Chapter 27. Deception 147

Chapter 28. The Dark Triad...153

Chapter 29. How To Analyze People..158

Chapter 30. Speed Reading to Understand People 166

Chapter 31. Advanced Tips and Tricks to Control People 174

Chapter 32. The Most Powerful Mind-Power Tool......................180

Conclusion 186

Introduction

NLP refers to the ability to sway interactions with other people. It has several different stages when used, beginning with establishing rapport and ending in getting the desired result. Ultimately, it is guided by non-verbal responses and reactions of the client, which can be used first to create rapport and sway the other person to do what is necessary.

NLP starts with developing rapport, which is typically done through mirroring and matching behaviors. You can cue the other person to begin identifying more with you when you use mirroring first. Following the other person's behaviors as a guide in interacting with him or her, you can begin keying into their desire to like you. They are more likely to identify with and trust you if you are mirroring them. It opens them up to the following step.

You will then be gathering information about the other person's mental state. It is using a study of body language or the way the other person may answer. When you understand the other person's mental state, you can begin understanding what their thought processes are, as well as the wording they use. It is where you start to understand the linguistic and programming parts of NLP. You can understand the other person's mind through understanding their words. You can begin to understand the mindset based on the wording, such as focusing on sensory-based metaphors or focusing on certain tendencies. You understand their programming by watching their body language with their words.

From there, it is time to start coming in on changing their minds. When the other person readily mirrors your interactions, you can begin speaking to the other person and mirroring the behaviors you want. For example, if you wish the other person to be more comfortable with spiders, you make a subtle body language sign that you are comfortable with when you mention spiders. You may learn in a little bit toward the other person, conveying that you are comfortable as you mention the spider. The other person should mirror your response, and as they do so, they tell their minds that there is nothing to fear, nothing to worry about, and that everything is fine.

This sort of process can then be expanded upon to be used for everything from depression to creating self-confidence in another person. It is, essentially, swaying the other person to feel more comfortable with things that may have been uncomfortable before. It allows you to sway opinions, behavior, goals, and more just by tuning into their body language, ensuring that you share rapport, and using that rapport to slowly mold the other person's mind to mimic the one you are attempting to create.

Historically, persuasion is rooted in ancient Greek's model of a prized politician and orator.

To make a list, a politician or speaker needs to master rhetoric and elocution to persuade the public. Rhetoric, according to Aristotle, is the "ability to make use of the available methods of persuasion" to win a court case or influence the public during important orations. On the other hand, elocution (a branch of rhetoric) is the art of speech delivery, including proper diction, proper gestures, stance, and dress. Although Grecian politics and orations seem clearly to be the genesis of persuasion, its use in the rapidly developing world of the twenty-first century goes beyond politics, oration, and other human endeavors.

In the business domain, persuasion refers to a corporate system of influence to change other people, groups, or organizations' attitudes, behavior, or perception about an idea, object, goods, services, or people. It often employs verbal communications (both written and spoken words), non-verbal communication (paralinguistic, chronemics, proxemics, and so on), visual communication, or multimodal communication to convey, change or reinforce a piece of existing information or reasoning peculiar to the audience. Persuasion in business can come in different forms depending on the need of the management. For instance, business enterprise sometimes uses persuasion in cases like; public relations, broadcast, media relations, speech writing, social media, client relations, employee communication, brand management, etc.

In psychological parlance, persuasion refers to using an obtainable understanding of the social, behavioral, or cognitive principles in psychology to influence the attitude, cognition, behavior, or belief system of a person, group, or organization. It is also seen as a process by which a person's attitude and behavior are influenced without coercion but through the simple means of communication. For instance, when a child begs his mother for candy and the mother refuses but instead proffers a better food for the child to eat while also encouraging him to grow more significant. The child gets excited and goes for the new alternative. In this way, the mother has been able to tap into his belief system without any form of duress. Hence, persuasion can also be used as a method of social control.

In politics and governing today, persuasion still retains its role as one of the essential means of influencing the populace's behavior, feelings, and commitment through the power of mass media. For instance, politicians sometimes use social media, television, radio, newspapers, and magazines to persuade people to sponsor their political campaigns. Persuasion in modern politics is also observed through the use of authority in such situations where opponents of one political party influence on cross carpet to the other party with different promises in the form of power and immunity. Also, the court still entertains the use of persuasion during the prosecution or defense of an accused.

Another way to see persuasion is through the intentional use of communication as a tool of conviction to change attitudes regarding an issue by transferring messages in a free choice atmosphere. The verbal, non-verbal, and visual forms of communication are manipulated just for the sole purpose of persuading an individual, group, or organization. Although communication is the most essential and versatile form in which persuasion is manifested, it is worthy to note that not all communication forms are intended to persuade. For instance, the celebration of a newly inaugurated president or governor circulated on the news cannot be classified as persuasion unless intended to impact the country's citizens or react in specific ways.

We go further to look at other possible definition of persuasion in the circular world.

Persuasion is a concept of influence that attempts to change a person's attitudes, intentions, motivations, beliefs, or behaviors. When a child begs his parent for candy and the parent says a big no to him, but the child insists on having candy even while knowing it might not be suitable for his health, persuasion is beginning to occur. The parent will try to proffer a better food for the child to eat instead of the candy. The child gets excited and goes for the new alternative. In this way, the parent has won a banter of persuasion.

On its own, persuasion is a branch of communication and popular as a method of social control. Hence, it is worthy of note that not all forms of communication intend to be persuasive. Persuasion is also a process by which a person's attitude and behaviors are influenced without harsh treatment by simple means of communication. Other factors can also determine a person's change in behavior or attitude, for example, verbal threats, a person's current psychological state, physical coercion, etc.

Having explained the meanings of persuasion, it can be observed that persuasion extends beyond a specific field as there is an intermingling of ideas from different study areas. However, communication and psychology seem clearly to be in use for persuasion to take place. While communication provides the model of how interlocutors in persuasion get messages understood, psychology provides the mental processes model during persuasion.

Now that we know both NLP and persuasion basics, we will now go more in-depth into detail about the subjects connecting to these two from this point and forward.

Chapter 1. Neuro-Linguistic Programming (NLP)

NLP is a fantastic art and science. It is an art since everyone gives what they are doing their own personal and stylish touch, which can never be conveyed with words or techniques. It is a science, and for outstanding results, there is a system and process to discover the models used for outstanding in-dividing in a region. This method is called patterning. In the field of education, guidance, and industry, the models, skills, and techniques discovered can increasingly be used to achieve more efficient communication, have substantial personal growth, and accelerate learning.

Have you ever done something so elegantly and successfully that your time will be cut short? Have there been moments when you were very pleased with what you were doing and how you handled it? The NLP shows you how to appreciate your achievements and arrange them to experience several more moments like this. It is a way of uncovering and unveiling your talent, a form of bringing out the best of yourself and others.

The NLP is a real ability that produces the outcomes we want in the world while at the same time valuing others in the process. It is the p of what distinguishes between the excellent and the nor-evil. It also leaves behind many extremely successful strategies on schooling, therapy systems, business, and therapies.

The History of NLP

The initial version of the NLP of today originated in the early 1970s. At the time, Richard Bandler was a student at the Santa Cruz University of California, met with John Grinder, assistant professor of linguistics.

Grinder, who was especially interested in advanced teaching techniques, was rapidly aware of Bandler's research and held a series of seminars in collaboration with him. Such seminars originally had the classification of group studies. But with growing Bandler and Grinder experience and expertise, the participants encountered more exciting transition processes ever. It culminated in an increasingly close relationship between Bandler and Grinder over the years.

They explored why well-known individual psychotherapists had so much success with their patients in their practice and on what basis this success was based. Several people treating the same patients with the same conditions have struggled to bring about these drastic improvements simultaneously. In Bandler and Grinder's original theory, they believed influential psychotherapists had a common or similar pattern of action in their work with people, based on which they might produce these excellent results. These standard or related behavior patterns are now known as NLP, or magic structure.

So, they started to investigate and evaluate the types of therapy used by the top therapists:

- Virginia Satir, an exceptional family therapist.

- Fritz Perl's, an innovative Gestalt therapist and founder of this direction of therapy, as well.

- Milton H. Erickson, a world-renowned hypnotherapist.

In doing so, the expectations of finding patterns and structures that could clarify these top therapists' success in coping with their clients were always driven.

Despite the three successful psychotherapists' diversity, after long and careful observation, Grinder and Bandler discovered that they used surprisingly similar basic patterns in their work with others. Grinder and Bandler put these basic patterns into writing, refined them, tried them out in their seminars with other students who agreed to do so. Finally, they developed an elegant model to achieve more effective communication, accelerated learning, personal change, and enjoyment, and joy in life. They called it NLP—Neuro-linguistic Programming:

"Neuro" because these are strategies that heavily involve the functions of our nervous system (brain + spinal cord + senses). The point is to perceive more precisely and more, to purposefully change unwanted feelings and behavior patterns in harmony with yourself.

"Linguistics" because it is also very much about the linguistic aspect. We maintain external communication with other people and internal communication with our fantastic "bio-computer"— our brain. Unfortunately, not all of the inputs that we make in this biocomputer are received. Therefore, advanced communication methods are also required here.

"Programming" means that we want to use systematic methods in all of this and not learn through trial and error. It's about discovering procedures and processes that can also be transferred to other areas and people. Many NLP techniques are content-free, which means that the same method can be used for headaches, a phobia, or to build an irresistible motivation. NLP describes procedures and processes that can and are effective regardless of the content.

Based on this approach, NLP developed in two complementary directions:

- In the first direction, as a process for discovering the pattern of brilliant achievements in every conceivable social area.

- The second direction is a compilation of effective ways of thinking and communication used by outstanding personalities in this field.

Beginnings of NLP

In the spring of 1972, Bandler himself offered a Gestalt therapy seminar, inspired by his studies' lack of real significance. It was possible for students in an advanced semester. He focused mainly on studying the therapeutic effects of gestalt work in a group and improving his theoretical skills in practice.

During these seminars, John Grinder became aware of Bandler's research, joining him and his exploration. From then on, both worked together on Bandler's workshops, with John Grinder, a beginner to counseling and psychotherapy.

Between 1972 and 1974, intense and productive cooperation took place, with Grinder benefiting from Bandler's knowledge of psychotherapy and Bandler's knowledge of linguistics.

This combination was particularly useful in modeling Virginia Satir's therapeutic masterpieces, Friedrich Perl's, and hypnotherapist Milton Erickson. When modeling, a person's unique skills are made learnable and accessible through systematic and accurate observation and questioning. Patterns and principles were developed so that interested people could also emulate the skills.

Bandler and Grinder were not primarily concerned with explaining something real but with discovering something useful for others. As proof of the success of their analyses and observations on Satir and Perl's, they saw evidence that in other people, they could achieve the same results as the person who modeled them.

In early 1974, both began designing the first meta-model structures with students held in Mission Street squat, Santa Cruz. To simply put, and the meta-model is a set of particular questions to uncover thinking processes and obtain in-depth knowledge. The starting point for research in the meta-model groups was that verbal communication between therapist and client is central to any therapeutic change work. Consequently, it was believed that common language patterns would crystallize and be cemented in Friedrich Perl's and Virginia Satir's verbal communication, making the dysfunctional processes conscious and causing change.

With John Grinder's linguistic context knowledge, both researchers succeeded in creating starting points for a model that allowed the targeted collection of information about a person's imaginary world. They modeled Perl's and Satir's critical linguistic skills and explained these constructs clearly and thus move them on.

From late 1974, Bandler and Grinder regularly participated in teaching seminars given by hypnotherapist Milton H. Erickson. Again, with the primary objective of researching Erickson's work with people, talking about his language patterns and actions. The findings were refined as with Satir and Perl's, reported in writing, tested for applicability in student groups, and integrated into the current knowledge base.

In 1974 and 1975, more formal communication models became the focus of group study. Since Perl's non-verbal actions often appeared to contribute significantly to the therapeutic impact achieved in addition to language behavior, the beneficial non-verbal elements were then specifically evaluated and attempted to address them. The resulting models were then used for both psychotherapy and daily contact.

Various types of procedures were used and revamped, leading, in addition to Perl's and Satir methods, to the current NLP shape. Bandler and Grinder published their first discoveries in four books from 1975 to 1977. These were:

In 1977, Grinder and Bandler held their first U.S. public seminars. The seminars were received very quickly. NLP's awareness has grown noticeably in the following years and is now used worldwide, especially in therapy, education, and management.

Bandler and Grinder developed reframing in 1982. It shows how one can contact unconscious parts, causing unwanted behaviors or disease symptoms. It enabled changes that were recently only conceivable under classical hypnosis.

1984 introduced the concept of submodalities, inventing one of NLP's most significant and impressive techniques. The submodalities represent a kind of brain programming language that everyone can use if they know the commands. People take information with their five senses, process it, and store it internally as events and thoughts represented in their senses, the so-called modalities. These modalities can, in turn, be specified more precisely, so it is possible to ask more precisely about an experience's inner picture. The fantastic thing about it is that it takes advantage of the fact that the human brain reacts to WHAT we think and how a person thinks, e.g., more in color pictures or black and white pictures.

James developed Time Line Therapy (Zeitlinie) in 1988. This method is particularly suitable for gently healing past traumatic experiences. Using the timeline, unconscious or repressed traumas causing physical or emotional problems can be found and mentally processed.

In 1990, Robert Dilts developed reimprinting to change our childhood's relational structures to limit beliefs and beliefs. An imprint is a decisive experience from which the person concerned has formed a belief or bundle of beliefs that are effective in his world. Such an imprint usually also includes an unconscious assumption of the role by other important people involved. The purpose of reimprinting is to find the missing resources, change the belief, and adapt the role model developed to the person's actual and acute circumstances.

Unlike popular belief, Grinder and Bandler did not create NLP alone. After thirty years of silence, a third colleague now goes public: Frank Pucelik.

Chapter 2. How NLP Works, Importance of NLP, and is NLP Effective?

How NLP Works?

If you are coming across this topic for the first time, NLP may appear or seem like magic or hypnosis. When a person is undergoing therapy, this topic digs deep into the patient's unconscious mind. It filters through different layers of beliefs and the person's approach or perception of life to deduce the early childhood experiences responsible for a behavioral pattern.

In NLP, it is believed that everyone has the resources that are needed for positive changes in their own lives. The technique adopted here is meant to help in facilitating these changes.

Usually, when NLP is taught, it is done in a pyramidal structure. However, the most advanced techniques are left for those multi-thousand-dollar seminars. An attempt to explain this complicated subject is to state that the NLP user (as those who use NLP will often call themselves) is always paying keen attention to the person they are working on/with.

Usually, many NLP users are therapists, and they are very likely to be well-meaning people. They achieve their aims by paying attention to those subtle cues like the eye's movement, flushing of the skin, dilation of the pupil, and subtle nervous tics. It is easy for an NLP user to determine the following quickly:

- The side of the brain that the person uses predominantly.

- The sense (smell, sight, etc.) that is more dominant in a person's brain.

- The way the person's brain stores and uses information.

- When the person is telling a lie or concocting information.

When the NLP user has successfully gathered all this information, they slowly and subtly mimic the client by taking on their body language and imitating their speech and mannerisms. They start to talk about language patterns that aim to target the client's primary senses. They will typically fake the social cues that will quickly make someone let their guard down to become very open and suggestible.

For example, when a person's sense of sight is their most dominant sense, the NLP user will use a very laden language with visual metaphors to speak with them. They will say things like: "do you see what I am talking about?" or "why not look at it this way?" For a person that has a more dominant sense of hearing, he will be approached with an auditory language like: "listen to me" or "I can hear where you're coming from."

The NLP user mirrors the body language and the other person's linguistic patterns to create a rapport. This rapport is a mental and physiological state that a human being gets into when they lose their social senses. When they begin to feel like the other person they are conversing with; it is just like them.

Once the NLP user has achieved this rapport, they will take charge of the interaction by leading it mildly and subtly. Thanks to the fact that they have already mirrored the other person, they will now begin to make some subtle changes to gain a particular influence on the person's behavior. It is also combined with some similar subtle language patterns, which lead to questions and a whole phase of some other techniques.

At this point, the NLP user will be able to tweak and twist the person to whichever direction they so desire. It only happens if the other person can't deduce that something is going on because they assume everything is happening organically or consent to everything.

In NLP, there is a belief in the need for nature's perfection of human creation, so every client is encouraged to recognize the senses' sensitivity and use them to respond to specific problems. NLP also believes that the mind can find cures for diseases and sicknesses.

Importance of NLP

NLP's effectiveness is focused on the idea that your mind and body are all the tools you need to improve your life and your world. It will help you to identify specific goals and act. And by analyzing your behaviors' changes, you can adjust them to produce better performance.

Some clinical studies suggest positive benefits to weight loss, reduced anxiety, and a healthy mood from Neuro-speaker programming. A specific investigation also reveals a positive impact on children's learning abilities with dyslexia, helping them improve their self-esteem by reducing their anxiety level. Here are the other importance or benefits of NLP:

As an adult, NLP lets you take responsibility for events that we feel we can't manage. A person can change his or her responses to past events and control their future through NLP. It is essential to be aware of people's body language in your inner circle and those you want to communicate with. NLP offers opportunities to use controlled and purposeful language. It helps you to monitor your life. With the same mind, you can't make the same mistakes and expect a different outcome. A Neuro-Linguistic (NLP) class is all about YOU; you are the subject. It is more important because it gives you more insight when dealing with individuals when dealing with yourself or yourself as an entity.

NLP helps you improve sales performance, income, health problems, better service to client, family, parenting, and all areas of your life. It allows you to become whole when your relationship with yourself and people is whole as an individual.

NLP helps you focus on your ideas, beliefs, and values. It allows you to understand your brain functions, how it develops patterns, how these behaviors become habits, how these habits become actions, and how these actions become outcomes.

The NLP application covers different professions and vocations in life. It is a highly competent tool for sales degrees, self-help and development experts, parents, teachers, communications, etc.

"You are all you ought to be, and all this is sufficient. Be proud of who you are and love who you are."

Is NLP Effective?

Based on valid, recognized, and established scientific research in sociology, linguistics, and psychology, NLP theories have been largely discredited as pseudo-science. The founders of NLP based their theories on sound scientific research. Still, the scientific community has repeatedly stated that the founders' comments and responses to inquiries have demonstrated that they do not understand the underlying theories they often cite in their work. Also, they have not produced any of their actual scientific evidence to support the claims made by NLP theorists or that their programming sessions bring about the changes they promise.

Mainstream psychology has established through clinical research, practice, and published works the reality of the subconscious mind and the importance of understanding its function to help alleviate, treat, or change harmful psychological developments in individuals. Cognitive-behavioral therapy (CBT) and traditional psychotherapy must meet with fairly rigorous professional standards and are based on proven methods and clinical psychology theories. At the same time, NLP's success record is less consistent and based more on anecdotal testimony.

NLP providers generally have a financial interest in promoting NLP's success, so their testimonials may or may not be accurate. Also, results among people who have completed NLP training sessions are mixed. Some studies have shown that patients who participate in NLP have improved psychological symptoms and a better quality of life. Still, most studies indicate little evidence that NLP can effectively treat any significant psychological disorders, such as anxiety, insomnia, or substance abuse.

However, while clinical studies have discredited NLP as a legitimate form of treatment for severe psychological illnesses, NLP continues to be part of the large, profitable industry that capitalizes on the demand for self-improvement literature. Tony Robbins, the contemporary self-help, self-improvement, and motivational speaking guru, trained with NLP's founders and continues to employ many of their ideas in his famous seminars.

Regardless of all the adverse press reports and scientific criticisms, NLP has spawned a global industry. Companies such as NLP Power, The NLP Center, The Empowerment Partnership, and the founders' own NLP University continue to advertise and promote their services on the internet and provide behavior modification training to a global audience. Many corporations and government agencies also send employees to NLP-based seminars to train leadership teams and sales staff. Thus, while the scientific foundations of NLP have been exposed and discredited, these organizations continue to attract followers and clients who see a benefit in the behavioral changes that result from associating with organizations that provide training in psychological and behavioral change.

Chapter 3. Components of NLP and NLP Techniques

Components of NLP

NLP's core philosophy is built on three essential components. From these components, other researchers and practitioners have expanded upon them. So long as these three components are respected, NLP is believed to work and be effective. To reach their maximum potential, practitioners need to pay close attention to how these pillars interact with one another.

Subjectivity

The first component, or core concept, is subjectivity. It is based on the fact that we all have different perceptions of the world around us. And while there are universal concepts that are believed and accepted, the fact of the matter is that we all have an experience that differs significantly.

Moreover, subjectivity is the basis of human experience. Therefore, we need to engage all of our senses to perceive the world as best we can. It is why educators who implement NLP seek to engage all five senses within the learning experience. That way, learners can get a good sense of the content they are trying to internalize.

Consciousness

NLP is predicated because the human psyche is built on a dual-layer of consciousness and unconsciousness. In this manner, the human psyche uses consciousness to express rationality for the things that we do daily. On the flip side, unconsciousness is the automatic manifestation of the built-in programming that we have accrued throughout your evolution.

Learning

Learning occurs when the conscious internalization of the world around us is achieved through the senses' perception. When a person can internalize content or their particular perception of the experiences they live, they can transform this into learning. It is why experience is crucial to the effectiveness of NLP. Unless a human is unable to experience the world, meaningful learning cannot fully take place.

NLP Techniques and How They Work

Neuro-Linguistic Programming (NLP) tells you that emotions and experiences guide people on their planet's view. It tells us that what you currently see isn't the critical world but a distorted representation supported your beliefs, perceptions, values, and other variables. NLP techniques will help you integrate aspects of your life, improve your quality, and understand how people work. Discover how to use these NLP techniques to enhance communication skills and emotional intelligence that you can use to regulate your life and mind.

Anchoring

The anchoring technique in NLP is important to tug up a particular emotion or put yourself into a specific psychological state, which may be used on yourself or somebody else. It works by integrating emotion with a physical movement, and the anchor laying dubs it. For example, if you decided to tug the thrilling feeling, you'd start by brooding about the days you have been euphoric. You'd wish to tell the account of what went on in your head that led to the present moment. Mention how it feels and enter an excellent deal of detail. Remember the instant, the emotions.

First, confine your right to your left index and middle fingers. Squeeze them twice. Mention your special moment on the second squeeze and strive to feature the feeling. Describe once more how you are feeling, how you think, and clap your hands twice. Let the nice and cozy feeling double once you clap the second time. Roll in the hay continuously for five times. You'll use those gestures to regain your feeling of happiness. You'd use a fast touch of the arm to secure them if you were to try this to a different man.

Meta Model

The methodology of the meta-model of NLP is usually wont to understand other individuals' concerns. It could even be wont to support others to possess a better understanding of their issues. The aim is to dismantle the conversation, assist you in achieving the basis explanation for the difficulty, and fix it. The response is consciously or unconsciously understood when someone features a question, but the only solution is some things that they are doing not like. The shortage of uncertainty allows the crisis to persist, anticipating that there'll finally be a replacement solution. You'll help them develop how by deconstructing the way someone explains their question.

Mirroring

One of the foremost relevant NLP strategies you ought to learn is mirroring. It'll be very beneficial to be good at mirroring. It's been quite hard to hate someone who knows the way to do that act. Moreover, it's the replication of the individual you interact with (i.e., his/her behaviors). While being subtle and typically subconscious, this simulation is complete. Copying somebody's speech patterns, visual communication, vocabulary style, speed, rhythm, pitch, voice, and volume are ways you'll do that.

Framing

The technique of NLP framing is employed to affect the rise or decrease of the emotional feeling significantly. It is an excellent way to use alongside most of the others. You are going to experience good and bad moments in life. These should enable you to be ready to learn and grow in your life. Nonetheless, memories haven't any feelings connected to them. Such separation occurs because memories and thoughts exist in several parts of the brain. Therefore, at present, you'll experience feelings, then you'll be ready to remember them. The hippocampus is that the brain part that's liable for LTM storage. The amygdala is the brain's portion that regulates feelings. The amygdala will offer you a fast-little reminder of what you feel once you recall a memory from the hippocampus. Simply because of that, the feeling that's important to a selected memory is often modified.

Pattern Interruption

Interruption of the pattern is usually wont to preserve words during a listener's subconscious. One great technique to pair with others is that this technique. To try this, you've got to draw the listener's thoughts into a series or pattern form. When the model gets out of control before finishing the shape, you would like to require them out of the template for a critical juncture. The listener's unconscious is meant to embody the pattern while the conscious mind is overwhelmed at that moment. You'll change the way you think that check out the past, and consider your life with a replacement way of thinking by learning NLP. It can help to enhance your communication skills and enhance your emotional intelligence.

Chapter 4. The Swish Pattern

The Swish Pattern is your answer to powerful and constant change. It is one of the most widely known and widely used NLP tools, and it helps people genuinely create their ideal self and eliminate negative behaviors. Using visualization, the Swish Pattern allows you to take the old images and behaviors you have developed over the years and replace them with powerful, dynamic. All-around better images and behaviors that work for the new ideal life you want to build.

First, though, you need to understand what visualization is:

Visualization

Visualization has gotten a bad rep, mostly because it has been tied up with Oprah's new age movement and the Law of Attraction. Everything can be yours if you just sit down and visualize that it is yours. And that is left behind many bitter and angry people who are ready to say visualization is not good. But, visualization is a tool used by athletes, politicians, and billionaire business people who want to get more and more from their life. Which is all to say many people are wrong.

One of the essential foundational tools for change when it comes to using NLP is visualization. To powerfully use all the NLP tools, you will need to understand what visualization is and how to use it, especially when using the Swish Pattern.

Power of Visualization

Dr. Biasiatto did a study at the University of Chicago, where he took three groups of people and tested their free-throw ability. He took note of each of their scores, and then he had one group practice their free throws for an hour every day for a month. The second group makes them visualize, making free throws for a little bit every day. In the third group, he had to do nothing at all.

In the end, the group that did nothing improved in no way whatsoever. The first group that practiced an hour a day improved their free throws by 24%. The visualization group was just 1% short of people who practiced for an hour a day. They improved at nearly the same rate as those practicing every day through merely the power of mental rehearsal.

Study after study has confirmed that the brain processes a visualized event the same way a real event happens. Athletes who visualize their playing see their muscle fibers activate and their brain process as if they are doing it. Some of the world's wealthiest and most influential people talk about using visualization to enhance their success, get better ideas, and achieve faster.

Visualizing is real. It works when you know how to do it. But, there are a few things that usually trip people up that do not have to trip you up. First and foremost, you do not have to be able to see anything. It is so important because many people think if they are not visual thinkers, then the visualization will not work for them, so they never try it.

Also, though, this will come if you practice visualization enough, your brain will learn to start creating images, and you'll feel a lot better about the whole process. But for many people, they are not visual thinkers, so they're initially just not seeing anything.

It's okay. You do not have to see anything to visualize (as weird as that sounds). Your brain will create experiences for you; if you focus on it, you will access other areas of your body, whether kinesthetic, verbal or anything else.

You will develop the feelings and the skills you are looking for. Now that you understand visualization, let us talk about the Swish Pattern.

The Swish Pattern

The Swish Pattern is a life changer that helps people with weight loss, smoking cessation, better habits, a healthy self-image, a more meaningful and better life. The thing is that you already have your ideal-self likely built inside of you. You know what your life would look like if you did not have your problems and what amazing things could happen with your life once those problems were solved.

You probably have a self-image of yourself that is far and away from your ideal, one that has been built by those problems weighing you down and working on you. It is these two images that you can leverage to make significant changes in your life.

Swish Pattern Step by Step

Step 1: Recognize Your Automatic Reactions

Images, thoughts, emotions, and a host of other things can cause you to have an adverse reaction. Whether you are reaching for a cigarette or a muffin, or it is making you yell and scream, or retreat and cower. We all respond to certain stimuli in remarkably consistent ways with our character that probably does not always help us be the best version of ourselves that we would want to be. You want to find that automatic response for whatever behavior or emotion or anything else that you want to fix. Once you do, you want to narrow down all the images, emotions, and anything else that forms in your mind when you respond in those automatic fashions.

You want to create an ideal image, a simple, powerful one that connects with your emotional state. It should be inspiring, exciting, and something that should make you want to change. You want to create this image focusing on your life would be like without whatever negative automatic response you have.

Once you have these two things, you want to create an image of yourself disassociated from both of these things, almost as if you're watching these two images from a distance, looking at them, admiring them.

Step 2: Determine the Cause of the Negative Image

As we said, you have automatic responses, and hopefully, you will have found them. Now, it is time to isolate what causes these automatic responses. Something brings these negative states to the forefront of your mind. Negative behaviors do not come from anywhere. Find that trigger. Ask yourself, "What Occurs Before This Negative State Begins?" This way, you can imagine the automatic response happening from the trigger and be prepared to create an alternative response to this event in the future.

Step 3: Prepare for Displacement

Take the positive image that you made initially, make it the size of a postage stamp in your mind, and place it on the corner of your developed negative image. You will want to notice a few things from its placement in the corner of the image. Its brightness, it is strength, and everything else that makes it stand out.

Step 4: Swish the Two Images

Now you are going to swish the images back and forth. Making a Swish sound can help because it gives your brain something else to engage with. Imagine the images switching places—the positive one growing more prominent, brighter, and more colorful. The negative one shoots off into the distance of your mind, disappearing and becoming nothing but a memory.

Notice how the further an image travels in your mind, the further the malicious behavior feels a part of you. More importantly, notice how, when the positive image gets brighter, your positive image can feel better.

Step 5: Repeat the Process

Keep repeating the swishing. Bring the old image back to the front of your mind; notice it as it loses color, as it gets blurry, as it begins to lose more and more of its power. You will notice the more powerful image continuing to glow brighter and brighter in the corner, almost as if it cannot be contained.

Keep the process going until the negative image has become tattered, black and white, blurry, and no longer packs the same emotions with it that it once did.

Step 6: Test It

Think about your negative emotion, think about the trigger, and find out if it is now replaced with that more powerful image that you want.

The Swish Pattern is a powerful tool, and it can completely liberate you from your negative behaviors and negative beliefs if you let it and you work it. It is there to help you genuinely transform how you live. You should notice improvement within a few days of using it, especially if you do it every day for a few days until it becomes part of your unconscious. There is no such thing as a transformation without actual work. You are going to have to work at it. The people who complain about the Swish Pattern do so because they thought they could do it once and forget it. But, that is not how it works. That is not how life works. But if you do it few a few days in a row, keep testing it; find where you're feeling weak with it. Within a week, you should see a clear improvement in your malicious behavior and see a positive transformation.

It works, and it works well. As you move through life, consistently trying to make yourself the best version of yourself possible, you will need to use this technique every time you want to end a malicious behavior. The more negative behaviors, beliefs, and emotions you can eliminate from your life, the better your overall life will be. The more you use this, the faster it will work, and the more powerful this technique will become in helping you create the behaviors and strengths you want in your life. You can install everything you want inside of you. You can make your life as exciting and memorable as possible.

The best thing about the swish pattern is that you can do it just about anywhere, and you can control the process. No need for audiotapes or some outside person guiding you through the process; no, you can be in complete control and have full power over yourself.

Start the process now and figure out what you want to change and what negative behaviors you want to eliminate from your life for good. Then create a list of desired behaviors and start to craft out everything that you want to do with your life and what your life will be like if you had these fantastic new behaviors instead of the negative ones you want to get rid of.

The more you design out your amazing future and your amazing life, the more you craft out the opportunity to create something marvelous for yourself to take over.

Chapter 5. Hypnosis

Hypnosis is a position of consciousness that involves focused attention, together with reduced peripheral awareness characterized by the participant's increased ability to respond to suggestions given. Every person has a waking state, a state when they know that they are awake, alert, alive, and in the universe.

What happens is that your attention becomes more and more focused, and your awareness of your environment diminishes. Your attention has more focused on what is inside and lesser on what is occurring outside. It makes you much more aware of your internal images, feelings, and thoughts and less aware of things going on in your surroundings. Usually, it's so pleasant for many people, enjoyable and very relaxing.

Highly imaginative people are usually easier to hypnotize: they have an intense experience of both nature and art. Psychopaths tend to be immune to hypnosis because psychopaths tend to have restricted emotions, but many people are easily hypnotized. Being in a hypnotic state is a regular aspect of human life. Often, creative people use guided imagination in their daily routine without necessarily realizing it as a hypnotic technique.

Three Stages of Hypnosis

Hypnosis is more of an ability than a disadvantage unless you are often hypnotically governed by an external force. Three stages are recognized in the hypnosis field:

Induction

It is the first stage involved in hypnosis. Before a subject undergoes full hypnosis, the subject is introduced to the hypnotic induction technique. For many years, hypnotic induction was used to put the participant into their hypnotic trance, but the definition has altered some modern times. Some of the non-state theorists have comprehended this stage a bit differently. Instead, the theorists understand this stage as the technique to enhance the subjects' expectations of what will happen—defining the role that they will play, getting their attention to concentrate on the right direction and any of the steps that are required to lead the subject into the appropriate direction of hypnosis.

Various induction methods can be applied during hypnosis. The most used method is the Braidism technique. The Braids technique has a few variations, like the Stanford Hypnotic Susceptibility Scale, which is the most applied research tool in the hypnosis field.

For you to apply the Braidism technique, you will have to follow the following steps:

- First, take any object that you can find bright, for example, a watch case, hold it between your middle, fore, and thumb fingers on the left hand. Hold the object somewhere above the forehead to produce a lot of strain on the eyelids and eyes. During the process so that the subject can maintain a fixed stare on the object at all times.

- Secondly, the hypnotist should then explain to the subject that they should keep their eyes often fixed on the object. The subject will also be required to focus theirs mindfully on the idea of that specific object. The subject should not be allowed to think of any other thing or let their mind wander, or else, the process will not be successful.

After some time, the subject's eyes will start to dilate. With some more time, the subject will begin to assume a wavy motion. If the subject involuntarily closes their eyelids when the fore and middle fingers of the right hand are carried from their eyes to the object, they are in a trance. If this is not the case, the subject will be required to start the process again: you should ensure that you let the subject know that they are to let their eyes close once the fingers are carried in a similar motion back towards the eyes again. It will get the subject to go into an altered state of the mind or hypnosis.

Suggestion

At first, the term suggestion was not used. Instead, Braid defined this stage as the act of having the conscious mind of the subject concentrate on one dominant and central idea. Braid did this to reduce or trigger the various regions' physiological functioning on the subject's body. Braid then started to emphasize applying various non-verbal and verbal forms of suggestion to get the subject into the mind's hypnotic condition. These would involve using waking suggestions as well as self-hypnosis. Hippolyte Bernheim, another hypnotist, emphasized the hypnosis process's physical condition over the psychological process that included verbal suggestions. According to Hippolyte, hypnosis is the induction of a physical state that is peculiar and which will enhance the susceptibility of the suggestion to the subject. He always stated that the hypnotic condition that is induced would assist in facilitating the suggestion.

Modern hypnotism applies various suggestions to be successful, such as direct verbal suggestions, insinuations, metaphors, non-verbal suggestions, and other figures of speech that are non-verbal. Some of the non-verbal suggestions that may be used would include mental imagery, voice tonality, and physical manipulation.

One of the distinctions made in the types of suggestions offered to the subject includes those suggestions delivered with permission and more authoritarian. One of the aspects that have to be considered regarding hypnosis is the difference between conscious and unconscious minds. Several hypnotists view this stage to communicate directed to most of the participant's conscious minds.

Susceptibility

It has been observed that people will react differently to hypnosis. Some will find that they can easily fall into a hypnotic trance and don't have to put much effort into the process. Others will find that they can get into the hypnotic trance, but only after a prolonged period and with some effort applied. Still, other people will find that they cannot get into the trance and, even after constant efforts, will not reach their goals.

One thing that has been found about the various subject's susceptibility is that this part remains unchanging. If you have gotten into a trance easily, you will likely be the same way for the rest of your life. On the contrary, if you have challenges teaching your hypnotic star of mind and have never been experiencing hypnotized, then it is probably that you never will.

Two types of victims are considered to be highly susceptible to the effects of hypnotism. These include:

- Fantasizers

- Associates

Fantasizers will have a high score on the absorption scales; they will block out easily the real world's stimuli without the use of hypnosis. They spend a lot of time daydreaming, they grew up in an environment where imaginary play was encouraged, and they had imaginary pals when they were in their childhood.

Associates will always come from childhood abuse or trauma; they found ways to forget their trauma and escape into numbness. When they daydream, it is more in terms of going blank instead of creating fantasies. Both dissociation and fantasizers score highly on the tests of hypnotic susceptibility.

Two groups of people with the highest hypnotism rates include those suffering from dissociative identity disorder and post-traumatic stress disorder.

Effects of Hypnosis

In a trance state, your ability to think logically and critically reduces. You tend to accept any information that is given to you without thinking if it's reasonable and rational or not.

People in a hypnotic state are suggestible. They tend to consent uncritically to any suggestions given to them. Even the strong-willed people can be hypnotized and made to do things that they wouldn't normally do.

Conscious decision making, independent judgment, and rational analysis are all suspended. It is a bonus for leaders who, after all, don't want their members thinking of themselves. Hypnosis is an incredibly powerful set of tools to influence others and manipulate others to do things that violate their ethics and morals.

What Manipulators Say

It is exciting that most leaders usually claim that people can't be made to do things against their will, even when applying mind control hypnosis.

The members are programmed to agree to whatever the leaders say. Therefore, the members will tend to accept the idea. Implicit in the idea is that if the person does something, they do it of their own volition.

When you make your own decisions, you believe more firmly and more committed to the outcome, and the actions and effects of your decision last longer.

Myths About Hypnosis

You should remember that hypnosis is not often a closed-eye process. It's not compulsory to have your eyes closed to be in a trance. Have you ever tried to be on a trip or journey, and when you reach your destination, you do not even remember much of the journey? That is an example of a trance that you were in.

People in a trance state who are driving while their eyes are entirely open and performing; if they see a person in front braking, there's no difficulty in braking themselves and doing what is necessary to avoid accidents. Many have the idea that there are unique hypnotic words to trigger trance. Hypnosis can be triggered in normal-sounding conversations, using the daily words.

Chapter 6. Brainwashing

If you talk to someone and ask them what they think brainwashing is, they may reply that they know because this is a topic that many people have heard about. But most people don't have a full understanding of how this kind of mind control can work. And if you are trying to fight off someone using dark psychology, you must make sure that you understand this topic.

Brainwashing will be the slow process of taking the ideas that a victim has about their identity and their beliefs and then replacing them with new ideas to suit the manipulator's purpose. Brainwashing can occur in a narrow and broad context. For example, a brainwasher could use the techniques to control one person or use those techniques to control a more extensive group's minds all at once.

The Process of Brainwashing

The starting point of brainwashing is the social circumstances and the mental state of the victim. It will be the basis for the rest of the process, and if the manipulator cannot figure this part out, then the brainwashing session won't be successful. Brainwashing is not a process that is going to work out for everyone. It will require an adequate identification of a person looking for something or someone who has a void they are trying to fill.

It brings us to an important point. Who is the ideal victim for a brainwasher? People who have had their existing reality shaken up because of some recent events are excellent brainwashers' targets. If you have lost someone you are close to or had another dramatic or traumatic event in your life, then you may be more susceptible to brainwashing.

Once the brainwasher has found their victim, the process of brainwashing can begin. Contrary to the popular image you may have in your mind about a brainwasher, this person will often come across as someone rational, friendly, and calm. Someone who seems to have their lives together in a way the victim wishes they could have their own. Visualize how it would feel if you were homeless and a celebrity you admired befriended you. It is often how the process of meeting the brainwasher is going to feel for the victim.

The brainwasher is going to get to work right away. The first step for them is to create a rapport and trust between them and the victim. It is going to be done with superficial and deep similarities. The superficial similarities could involve some surface-level preferences, something like enjoying the same food or sport as the other person.

They will then move on to a deeper level of rapport, some that could involve a more in-depth shared experience that they had in the past. The brainwasher will most likely fake these, convincingly, to create these bonds. If the victim shares with the brainwasher that they lost a close relative in the past, then the brainwasher is suddenly going to have a similar story to share with the victim.

This false connection and warmth emotionally are not the only thing that is going to occur. The brainwasher wants to cement that new bond as quickly as possible. It is not unconventional for them to provide favors and gifts to their victim. They could send them a gadget or some other item they may find useful. They may treat the victim to a meal. It is to create a sense of gratitude and indebtedness from the victim to that brainwasher. It is going to soften up a lot of the resistance that the victim may experience.

After the resistance has been stripped away a little bit, the other step will be a sort of romantic presentation. It will involve the brainwasher slowly and increasingly offer a solution to any problems that the victim recently opened up about. It is not going to be a big hard push or sell. Instead, the brainwasher knows how to do this in an offhand and casual way to make sure they don't deal with any negative experiences by pressing the victim. This solution will always be the personality, ideology, or cult that the brainwasher is working to make the victim convert.

When these steps are done correctly, the initial stages will leave the victim wanting more. The victim will want more information and more understanding of the solution that the brainwasher hints at. The brainwasher may even withhold some of this information initially, treating it as something that the victim needs to do some work to attain. Doing this is to push the victim to seek out and accept the information they are eventually going to hear.

After the victim has had some time being spoon-fed snippets of this belief system, and they have shown they will respond well to them, the brainwasher will be careful to reveal the right information at the right time. It is a concept that is called a gradual revelation or milk before meat. It will include the presentation of an easy to accept idea before the controversial idea is revealed.

For example, if the brainwasher is trying to convert the victim over to religious terrorism, they would not start with the terrorism part. They may initially start focusing on the fact that God loves the victim, something that the victim is likely to accept. The more objectionable ideas, such as God wants you to blow yourself up, are ones that are saved until much after in the process. Once the victim has accepted that last part, then this brainwashing session is at a point of no return.

In this situation, you may be curious why the victim is still engaging with the brainwasher, especially when these more objectionable ideas become apparent. There are three main reasons:

The brainwasher has worked on the vulnerable victim. They feel a strong sense of liking the brainwasher, and they want to get the brainwasher's approval.

The victim has invested some time, and in some cases, money, in the process up to this point. It is often known as the sunk cost fallacy. The victim will feel like it is terrible to throw away all the hard work and money they have put into the process.

During this process, the brainwasher has been amassing many sensitive and secretive information on the victim. The brainwasher is often willing to hold this information over the victim to keep the victim on the right path.

The Impact of Brainwashing

The above analysis that we did about brainwashing is going to show how severe this technique can be. It is changing the victim's beliefs and inner identity, and this can be a big deal. Sure, the manipulator will get what they want out of the process, but the victim will lose out on their real identity and often gets so far into the process that they aren't sure what went wrong.

Many different impacts will come with brainwashing after the process is completed. The first one is a loss of identity. Many ideologies and cults feature that the people who go through the initiation process are given a new name. It helps the psyche of the person to detach from their old identity altogether. They can believe things and even do things they would never have done in the past because that older adult they were no longer exists. When this process is carried out the proper way, it can leave a victim feeling like all the parts of their old identity are no longer real or permanent and that they have woken up from a nightmare.

Post-traumatic stress disorder, or PTSD, can sometimes be a hallmark of those who managed to escape or rescued from a situation where they were brainwashed. The victims of these brainwashing endeavors will show some of the same psychological and physical signs as war veterans who were right in the battle. The severity of this traumatic aftermath shows that this type of process, of the manipulator getting more control over the victim, could harm the victim as much as if they went to war.

Brainwashing is something that can have a lasting impact. There are plenty of examples of rescued individuals or who managed to escape from their brainwashing situation, who then went back to that situation of their own free will. Even when they were able to leave the brainwashing and controlling environment they were in, the legacy that came with that process was done so well and ran so deep in their mind that the victim wants to return to it. It shows the power of using this brainwashing process and how much a manipulator could gain.

Chapter 7. How to Use NLP for in Sales

We are all on sale, believe it or not. When was the last time you had to sell an idea you had to your boss or your colleagues or make a proposal to increase your project budget? When was the last time you had to convince your kids to do something they were supposed to do? Whether you sell a product, service, concept, or influence others to achieve the desired result, you sell.

The following 5-step sales process seems to be a simple framework to use and remember:

- Establish and maintain a rapport.

- Understand your client or potential client.

- Define the need/define the value.

- Need/value link to your product or service.

- Close the sale.

Neuro-linguistic Programming is the study of excellence and excellent communication and how to reproduce it. Your ability to communicate effectively is the key to your success in any business interaction. So, let's look at each step of the 5-step sales process and see how NLP fits in.

Establish and Maintain a Rapport

Keeping eye contact while talking or listening to another person is one way to stay connected. Leaning or bending forward and tilting a bit your head to the side while listening shows that you are entirely listening and engaged to the person you're talking to. Uniting and reflecting body, voice, and words is another way to create and maintain relationships. Any resistance you encounter means that you have not established enough relationships and an excellent indicator to go back and build an additional connection. Making a rapport is the first step to getting better results in sales or any communication interaction.

Understand Your Client or Potential Client

The best way to understand your client or prospect is to ask many open questions. Asking questions will allow you to know your client/potential client better and will allow you to identify if it is necessary for your product or service. Find out what is important to them, how they think and process information. Observe their eye patterns as they answer questions to see where they are going to access private information. Look at the main words you use most often. Do they prefer visual words and descriptors such as "I see, can I imagine," or do they incline to the auditory words "I hear what you think," "it sounds true." Or are they more appropriate with kinesthetic phrases like "I understand what you are saying"? I feel your passion. "If you understand the needs of the client or potential client and understand their communication style and preferences, you will be better prepared to communicate with them in a way that works best for them.

Define the Need/Define the Value

Once you have determined the need, you need to define a value. Do you realize it would be useful to solve your problem or improve the situation? Reinforce your value proposition by asking something like, "So it would be useful to answer that, right? Is it something that would interest you or not?" It is an important problem because they may have a need but see no value in solving it. Most sellers spend 80% of their time on people who don't buy. You want potential clients/buyers to buy while ensuring that the value solves their problem is crucial to your sales pitch.

Connect Need/Value to Your Product or Service

You don't sell a product or service in the sales process. You sell emotion. We believe it is our sound mind that makes the decision, but the fact is that all of our memories, feelings, and emotions are stored in our unconscious. Furthermore, the more significant part of our choices is made subliminally. Connecting with your client or client's sentiment is the key to your ability to close a sale successfully. For example, potential buyers looking to buy a new home can see the value of a locker room. You associate it with the sensation she will feel when she wakes up in the morning, approaches her, and feels good when she sees and chooses clothes quickly in the morning. This feeling will connect her to the house they are selling.

Close

If you have successfully followed steps 1 through 4, closing should be smooth. Just ask for a purchase or order. Take advantage of the sale to the end and look for a win-win opportunity.

Chapter 8. How to Use NLP in Relationships

In this part, we will know how NLP can be beneficial to healthy relationships. We will learn what excellent and fulfilling relationships are based on and built upon. We will explore techniques that can strengthen relationships and those that can help us establish healthy relationships. We will talk about the benefits or importance of our mental health and readiness before entering any partnership or relationship and possible outcomes associated with having and not having these factors.

Once you have decided what you want, now is the time to enter into a relationship and have covered your predetermining factors. Now you can begin to open up to the possibilities of finding the right person. Here is when rapport becomes essential. What is rapport? It's your similarities and likeness with someone you are interested in entering a relationship with. It's also the establishment of trust with that person. With rapport, many individual factors can be used for determining compatibility. Some of these are personality types, values, beliefs, culture, political ideologies, interests, religious beliefs, etc. Of course, physical characteristics, such as gender and body types, need to be considered. However, some features can't be overaccentuated because it will mimic the other and cause a loss of rapport.

The rapport established initially, the reasons for your attraction to your partner, and his or her attraction to you must be kept at the forefront of each partner's mind throughout the relationship. It all too familiar for people to enter relationships with guns blazing, meaning being the perfect partner, only to begin to relax and change once the relationship has been established. One partner, or both, will use all available techniques to get the other to enter into a relationship. Once they are in that relationship, the other partner believes they can initially tone down what they were doing. It is one of the typical reasons for relationships ending. Keep in mind, the reasons for someone falling for you are the same reasons that will make them want to stay with you. If you remove the reasons for their attraction, they have no reasons to stay with you. Often, we see children born of relationships used as new reasons, but this does not work. It leads the partnership to morph into, what be, a business relationship. There will be no real emotional connection in the relationship and, even though that couple may remain together, they will lack the comforts and fulfillment of needs they desire.

Now you have identified what you want, making sure the timing is right, and have met that special someone. Now, what do you do? You need to ensure that your significant other feels the same about you. There are several ways in which a person can see that they are loved by the other. These ways should be identified at the relationships beginning. A few methods are by what the other person buys and places he or she takes you. There are also things such as how they touch you, the looks they give, or what they say. Identification of these is essential as they can gauge the continuance of love throughout the relationship.

The best way to determine how you can best assure your partner that you love them is by doing what they tend to do for you. For instance, if your partner puts her arm around you at times to assure you of her love and affection, you can bet that if you do the same, she will believe that you do love and appreciate her. We don't tend to do things to or for others, especially those whom we care about the most, that we wouldn't want to be done to us. Although this is commons sense, it's also an excellent method to gauge or determine how your significant other feels about you. As the relationship progresses, this will come naturally and will take much less conscious effort. Be sure not to allow these things to stop just because the relationship is no longer new.

NLP has devised a few strategies to determine areas in relationships. Areas such as attraction, love, and desire are all strategized with NLP techniques. First, you must know your partner. It means that you should know what those subtle gestures and tones of voice your partner will display depending on how they feel. Know what your partner fears and what he or she wants. You will pick up ideas as to how to carry these things out by merely learning your partner. Be sure never to use this knowledge for manipulation. There isn't a positive outcome in relationships where manipulation takes place.

One technique you can use to ensure that your partner is in love with you and wants you is to remove yourself from his or her presence temporarily. It does not mean that you can tell your wife that you are going to the store for a lottery ticket to not return for a week. However, in short time frames, absence can signal want or lack thereof. Just like the cliché, absence makes the heart grow fonder; this is built on the same premise. When using these kinds of tactics, please never overuse them. Here is some advice. If you are an insecure person needing constant approval and reassurance that you are loved, you should take care of that issue before entering a serious relationship. If not, you will not be the right partner. If your shortcoming does not end the relationship, it could lead it to become a codependent partnership or, at the very least, a very unhealthy relationship. Again, you must first make sure that you are the right candidate for entering into a relationship before taking that other step.

With relationships, you are not merely selling yourself to another, and then the job is over. It's a continuing process forever. Never relax and believe that you have your partner and aren't going anywhere, no matter what you may or may not do. You should always be selling yourself, your worth, compassion, and desire for your partner.

Think of this; You meet someone at the beach or any spot you can imagine. You are both at that exact place at that same time. You may both have everything in common too. However, both you and the other person took different routes to that spot and lived through different circumstances while on the way. Even though you both find yourselves to be at the same point and with the same characteristics, you took different paths there. It means that it's likely that you are not both going to react or respond to every event the same, and those events may lead you to go in different directions. Another way to look at this; you may both like the same sports team. The difference is why each of you has this opinion of that team. One of you may be a graduate from that university, while the other just picked last season's champions. It probably means that the school's alumnus is less likely to decide that they no longer favor that team. Regardless of the possible ways, the ending remains the same. What does this mean? Are we all just merely at life's mercy and subject to emotional trauma at the drop of a hat? Not exactly. Although we may not be able to change the situation when finding ourselves here, we can know why. First, don't give up. Do whatever you can to carry both you and your partner through the tough spot in your relationship, and you may find that you both were able to beat the odds and remain together.

Let's look at what it means to have taken different routes. The recently mentioned scenarios were only metaphors. The location isn't an actual place but a specific state of mind and life situation. Regardless of the spectrum of commonalities you and your partner may or may not have, you both will respond and react to things differently. One of you may be able to brush something, such as a traumatic event, off, but the other cannot do that. Let's look at this. Both you and your wife have religious faith. It is one of the main commonalities you found of yourselves that led to your relationship. Then down the road, your wife either endures a traumatic event or meets an influential person, either causing a dramatic shift in her religious ideologies. What was once the main glue that kept you together has deteriorated to where there is no more left. Not only does she no longer agree with your religious faith, but her newfound beliefs also contradict what you believe. What do you do when faced with this situation? Both of you are firmly holding to your individual beliefs and not willing to waiver. Both accuse the other of being naïve. Neither of you is terrible people, but you are no longer finding the same rapport you once had.

You both joined the relationship only after taking the proper steps and exercised due caution in choosing the other as a mate. Even though this was done, life didn't care about that. Circumstances led to the separation of you and your partner's beliefs, and both of you are much too committed to your independent ideas to compromise them. Therefore, you are now at constant odds, and the negativity within the relationship grows stronger each day. One day, it will lead to resentment and even hate. You have taken the necessary steps in attempting to salvage the relationship to no avail. So, as the very last resort, you decide to part ways. It happens every day.

Like the baggage we carry due to prior bad relationships, we have lessons learned and unique ways of dealing with specific issues based on these lessons. The best thing to do is know what and how things are going, and this can give you a good idea as to what is about to come.

To conclude this guide, NLP is essential and beneficial in the relationship. It isn't just with the beginning of the union but throughout its entirety. You must first know yourself, and then using NLP; you can learn your partner. Knowing your partner can prove invaluable in maintaining a healthy and long relationship. Also, the relationship will be much more fulfilling to both parties. Remember that severe and personal relationships prove beneficial in many areas in life and isn't limited to just the partnership. It's beneficial for both of you as a couple, as individuals, and as part of society.

Chapter 9. NLP in Business

NLP enhances negotiation skills and selling skills. Clients who use NLP in the business report that their managers are excellent coaches, motivators, and influencers.

NLP multiplies excellence in any field. It is a skill known as modeling in NLP; it incorporates all other intermediate skills. It is beneficial in a business organization if, for example, business took good employees from each field and brought them together. The work done will be excellent.

NLP helps to improve communication while doing business. During communication, there is the use of verbal and non-verbal cues. Using NLP, one will be able to understand the spoken and unspoken language of clients and prospects.

It helps one to emulate the successful efforts of other businesses easily. NLP teaches one to understand how successful people work and converse. One can then emulate those using NLP strategies to copy those successes to fit their businesses.

NLP gives one sales staff mind-reading abilities. It enables them to understand non-verbal cues and eye movements, allowing them to answer clients' questions and provide useful information about the products. They also understand how a client feels about the product in question, making it easier for them to close sales.

NLP improves negotiation skills. Negotiation is a critical requirement in the business world—negotiation with vendors, employees' marketers, advertising firms, and many more. With

NLP negotiation skills, everyone in the business will be more effective and persuasive.

NLP boosts morale. Why wouldn't one's morale be boosted if everyone in the company or office knows how well and effectively you communicate? One can make themselves apparent as well as able to relate with everyone in the office. It makes the workplace much more fun since there is a better understanding of one another.

NLP is the best client service tool. NLP helps to understand clients' complaints and suggestions after a sale. One can discern if a client is complaining because of awful client service or if he or she is having a bad day. When one's client care can understand the client's non-verbal cues, he will be able to deal with the angry client and make them happy to come again.

NLP can be so useful in boosting your entrepreneurial pursuits. It helps build skills in teamwork, coaching, sales, productivity, personal development, and leadership. For NLP to be useful, there must be potential for growth, and human interaction should be present.

NLP is a useful tool when you are setting and working toward achieving your goals. When you are in a business state, you must set your goals, which are supposed to be achievable, intelligent, meaningful, and measurable. For instance, it will not be realistic for you to set a goal to earn millions of dollars within a month without having logical ways to achieve your goal. Thus, using NLP, it is possible to set and achieve goals for your business. Using NLP will help you change your way of thinking and speaking and motivate you to take appropriate actions toward achieving your goal.

When you are in a business, sometimes you become stressed, but if you apply NLP techniques, it is possible to have a happier and more fulfilling life. NLP includes studying successful people's steps to achieve success, and these successes can come out from any part of your body. These techniques will help you overcome phobias, speak with confidence in front of a large congregation, reduce anxiety, and learn how to be in a healthy personal relationship.

Brain Training Success Techniques

Avoid using weak words, such as try. The type of language you will use in your business matters, and you should avoid using vague language. "I will try to get that book tomorrow"—this sentence is not exactly whether you will do it or not. In a business, make your intentions clear, and avoid giving your clients unclear expectations. When dealing with your clients, only use action-based and positive language.

Away from or Move Toward

We all experience problems and obstacles as we move toward success. The way you tackle those problems matters. If you use NLP techniques, it becomes easier. Entrepreneurs have a way of solving their problems. They tend to break tasks, and then they apply logic to it. Then they look at it objectively by removing emotions from that particular problem. You are supposed to move toward the positive "I am capable of doing this. Although it is a difficult job, it is worth it.' And get away from negativity: "This is impossible. I am not able to do this difficult job."

Direction and Focus

NLP helps you use personality to create focus and direction from both a personal and professional perspective, perfect for direct reports in a coaching setting. It involves having an overview of different areas of both life and work, and this helps you have priorities and identify areas of neglect or drift. It enables us to agree to measurable objectives and actions, sharing benefits to both the individual and the organization.

Improving Personal Effectiveness

Improving personal effectiveness is effective in changing the long-term behavior of a person in the workplace. When employees understand one another, it becomes much easier to respond to one another's and the clients' desires and needs. It has been proven that well-functioning and healthy relationships are essential for success in one's personal life.

In conclusion, applying NLP techniques in your business will make you more successful. It is one of the exciting approaches to your problem, and it is worth trying. It improves your way of thinking and helps you achieve your goals.

How to Use NLP to Gain More Wealth and Get Better Results

It is every human being's wish to gain wealth and receive better results in life. We have different ways of doing so, and by using NLP techniques, it is possible to achieve that. These techniques help you to realize yourself and also the best way you can improve your earnings. Those ways are below.

One Can Make Money Using NLP, Using Various Methods

You Can Make Money with NLP as a Coach

Being a coach has many benefits. One can work from anywhere, work at their time, and work at their pay and price. Coaches help clients integrate their desired outcomes, set timelines and deadlines. Create goals, make them achievable, give advice, make the client see things that they cannot see by themselves, and help them stay accountable for what happens to follow up on what is happening.

One Can Also Make Money with NLP as a Practitioner

NLP gives you a tool to work well with people and almost everything that might be bothering them. It has been discovered that most people are looking for NLP practitioners, and one is very marketable. Being a practitioner helps people to:

- **Conquer fear and phobias**

They have different ways of helping people to overcome fear. Sometimes they expose their clients to what they fear most but in a safe and controlled environment. You will realize that you will learn how to combat your anxiety and fear, and after some time, you will be able to control it. Another way they use is teaching their clients the relaxation technique, which will help control both mental and physical feelings of fear. Some practitioners will suggest you seek medical help if you want to treat phobias, and after taking medication, that phobia will go away. Now you can live in everyday life.

- **Lose excess weight**

They usually suggest methods for us to lose weight. These methods include exercising and always practicing healthy diet habits. You are very aware that if you have too much weight, it can lead to you getting diabetes, affecting your everyday life.

- **Quit bad habits**

Habit is defined as a pattern of behaviors acquired through repetition. We have two categories of habits: good and bad habits. These bad habits make us not live a normal life, and this affects our productivity in life. These bad habits include smoking, gambling, etc. Smoking affects our life as nicotine found in cigarettes makes us addicts, and thus, for your body to operate normally, you have to smoke. There are several ways we can break these habits, but it varies from one person to another. It is broken using the following tips:

- **Identify the trigger.** It is the first step when you want to break the habit. Triggers include those things that go through your mind at that exact time. For example, reflect on what always goes through your mind when you are biting your nails.

- **Then try to replace bad behavior with a healthy one.** For instance, if you want to counteract smoking, try to find a new hobby you can practice during free time.

- **Avoid temptations.** Sometimes habits may be linked to a particular place or people. To break the habit, you have to avoid those friends, for instance, who are always drinking or gambling. That way, you can break the bad habit of drinking alcohol.

- **Keep your focus.** When you want to break a bad habit, you have to stay focused and committed to that. You should keep in mind that you are cutting the bad habit for your good. For instance, when quitting smoking, you are supposed to know that you are doing that to avoid getting diseases like cancer.

- **Never lose hope.** Hope is a pillar that keeps us moving. You should consider that you will face many obstacles when you are trying to leave a habit. Thus, you should have a plan to counter that if it arises. Do it once per day, and never give up.

- **Reward yourself.** When you stay away from a bad habit even one day, treat yourself. You buy yourself a new outfit, or you take a vacation. It will motivate you to keep avoiding the bad habit even though you are the one rewarding yourself.

- **Enhance confidence.** Sometimes we face situations that help us become confident. For instance, when you are having a staff meeting, confidence should be displayed. Practitioners help us boost our confidence by assisting us in identifying our weak points and strong points.

Here, people tend to confuse this with being a coach. A coach is different from a consultant in that a coach doesn't tell people what to do but helps clients find answers to their questions while consultants give specialized advice. For example, a business consultant helps his clients with concrete advice on how to grow their businesses.

You can also make money with NLP as an author. NLP training incorporates accelerated learning, NLP subconscious teaching principles, and layered learning. Becoming a published author increases one's credibility in the field, which will allow you to charge expensively.

You can also make money with NLP as a speaker. It again points to the knowledge one would have acquired from NLP. Suppose one continues with training beyond being a practitioner. In that case, they have the chance to enter a Master Trainer Development Program, where they issue all useful materials one requires to become a good speaker.

Chapter 10. Body Language and Behavior Imitation

Our non-verbal, or body language, is one of the most powerful communication methods we use in our day-to-day experiences. It is the mode of contact that ignites feelings and reactions on our "healthy point." Research has shown that understanding body language improves one's potential to effectively get out of any given situation, whatever one wants.

Have you ever encountered a couple sitting together and got a feeling of exactly how good or bad their friendship was in minutes? Have you ever questioned how you could arrive so quickly at this point without any prior interaction? Whether you are aware of it or not, we spend our days listening to people's non-verbal signals interpreted by their body language and drawing conclusions from our assumptions about them.

The body language shows that we conceal from the world in words and how we feel about ourselves, our relationships, and our circumstances. The individuals we associate with will evaluate our motives. The strength of our interactions, how masterful we are in any particular situation, our level of trust, and our real goals and aspirations by our eye contact, movements, body posture, and facial expressions.

The strength of body language is seen in the resulting emotional reaction. In nearly any case, emotions influence choices and reactions. Non-verbal signals activate emotions that define an individual's core properties, such as truthfulness, trustworthiness, honesty, competence level, and willingness to lead.

Understanding these signals will decide who we are going to meet, the work we are being recruited for, the amount of recognition we are having, and even those elected to powerful political positions.

Why do we not spend years studying and improving successful body language skills for such an immense skill? The fact is that most people undervalue the meaning of body language before they try a better interpretation of human conduct in an intimate relationship or in a competitive market situation to achieve an advantage.

Mastery in body language contains the keys for individuals to perceive the context of particular movements and body expressions and understand how to convey and express signals while communicating with others properly. As a result, there is a significant improvement in the general success of public interactions. The easiest way to continue this learning cycle is to study the simple understanding of the two core body language styles—open presence and closed presence.

The closed presence's body language form is illustrated in individuals who fold their bodies around the body's centerline, which runs straight down the middle of the body from the top of the head to the foot. The physical features that produce this form of appearance are feet positioned beside each other, arms held tight to the chest, hands folded across the chest, slight hand movements kept close to the body, shoulders rolling forward, and eyes fixed below eye level.

The world's signals transmitted by the body language form of closed appearance were a loss of confidence, low self-esteem, impotence, and lack of experience. In extreme cases, the message of needing to be invisible may also be produced. The consequences of this kind of body language on the person expressing can range from actually not having the best possible opportunity to a worst-case situation of harboring a self-fulfilling image of victimization.

By comparison, the accessible appearance is displayed in individuals that build a sense of dominance, control, and leadership by projecting mastery of confidence, achievement, energy, and ability. The physical features include feet held hip apart, freehand movements used in speech away from the body's middle line, elbows held away from the chest, shoulders pulled back, upright postures, and eyes fixed on their listeners' eye level. Such people are viewed as desirable, competent, intellectual, and are quickly seen as achieving success. We consider this form of body language as the "leaders' body language."

The aim is eye contact to enhance body language and to start expressing a transparent appearance. Face contact is one of the social devices that we enjoy most. Someone will alter the way others see them by making direct eye contact while communicating with others. Once people start looking straight into a victim's eyes, they are perceived as confident, trustworthy, and professional.

Hand gestures and facial expressions are the second degrees of improvement that one can create for a transparent face to be seen. Both methods of communicating improve the ability to and accurately convey information. Through skillfully using open hand motions away from the body and expressive facial expression, greater emphasis is produced when communicating through engaging the audience more physically and increasing the amount of knowledge provided during the conversation.

Body language mastery is essential to creating the most powerful presence in all human relationships. Individuals lacking this knowledge are vulnerable to confusion and find their attempts inadequate in expressing their thoughts. With the ability to distinguish between the various body language styles, everybody will achieve the competence required to excel in whatever pursuit they want.

Know and Understand Your Body Language

If you know it or not, body language is a significant force responsible for how everyone you encounter comes up with an opinion on you. Listening skills are a must and very necessary in many careers—particularly in careers where you support others to build positive relationships with clients. Whether you help people maintain their relationships, give people advice for business success or educate people about some other form of issue, they see your body language; displaying strong listening skills makes people feel relaxed.

Poor body language could result in something big being lost in you. It doesn't matter to you! Attentively and sincerely listen to every single word. It is the body language that makes you feel necessary to you and gives them the support they need. Understanding what the signs of a lousy listener are here is significant, and you will seek to rid yourself of all of these. When you have the habit of having your arms crossed around your stomach, whether you tap your feet impatiently, move whether turn and look away too much, or while listening, you tell the other person you're not interested in what he or she does. It will most likely lead to the termination of the partnership, which may cause significant business losses.

Ok, what would you do to continue transmitting constructive messages through your body language to the person you're talking to? You will first try to face the other party squarely on. Look not out to give a constructive signal. So at the moment of contact, we fall into the body's posture. You will take a transparent approach. You never have to leave your arms or legs folded; otherwise, the other guy would think you're not interested in listening to his point.

When you lean over when you speak to someone, your body language suggests you pay more attention to what he or she does. Leaning forward, by comparison, suggests you have little confidence whatsoever. The most pivotal aspect is eye touch. Seek to keep eye contact at all times. When you are looking down or turning down, it shows you have no interest in the topic and feel embarrassed.

However, the importance of a confident stance cannot be overlooked either. You don't want to be too uptight. You need not be too formal when talking to anyone, either. When you believe you have experienced significant defeats in the past due to your bad body language, you can instantly start following the above tips.

Behavior Imitation

Behavior imitation is something that can be used for good and for bad. Often, as children, we mimic the behavior of the people around us. It helps us to learn social norms. Also, it helps us feel like we fit into the crowd. Many traditions have been built off of people mimicking other people's behavior.

As we continue to grow up, we continue to imitate the people around us. Here again, it makes us feel as if we belong. Also, it can help us build relationships and understand the people around us more easily. While many people use behavior imitation for the right reasons, many others don't.

Criminals who are socially awkward tend to act like the people around them. It can make it harder to discern the good guys from the bad guys. It is a manipulation tactic that works quite well when people don't know how to behave appropriately. While some people are very good at mimicking those around them, it will be obvious when others try to do this. Cases of extreme social awkwardness will not allow the person to behave like those around them genuinely. It can be a tip to seeing what they may have planned after.

Another way that behavior imitation is prevalent with criminals is when they idolize someone or something. They will change their very persona to reflect that of which they admire. An excellent example of this is people that still follow the ideals of Adolf Hitler. The new generation of Nazis mimics the ways of old because they still believe his blasphemous thoughts to be true. It is truly scary behavior imitation.

Chapter 11. Using NLP to Manage People

When it comes to managing people effectively, it's essential that you first understand the non-verbal cues they provide to apply your skills toward influencing them. It is a necessary principle in using the NLP technique. Following are a few NLP techniques that can allow you to influence people's perception and thinking:

Deciphering Eye Movements

It is essential to realize and know the meaning of eye movements because each eye movement tells its tale. For instance, when searching for the right word or trying to remember a name, you automatically move your eyes in a certain way (most likely, squinting). Rolling the eyes signals contempt or exasperation.

Winking Indicates Flirtation or a Joke

Widening the eyes signals surprise or shock, even extreme excitement. The eyes can reveal much more about people's mental and emotional status, all on their own.

Once you understand what other people's thought processes are, you can accurately follow a course of action or dialogue which acknowledges the unspoken response, as signaled by the eyes. And as you may know, eye movements complement other communication forms such as hand movements, speech, and facial expressions.

Dilation of the pupils, breathing, angle of the body, and the hands' position—all these are complementary to the spoken message. Still, eye movement is essential in communication because every movement is influenced by particular senses and different parts of the brain.

Here is how you can generally interpret eye movement:

Visual Responsiveness

- **Eyes upward, then towards the right:** Whenever a person tilts eyes upward and then to the right, it means that the person is formulating a mental picture.
- **Eyes upward, then towards the left:** Whenever a person tilts eyes upward, followed by an eye movement to the left, it means the person recalls a particular image.
- **Eyes looking straight ahead:** Whenever someone focuses directly in front of them, this indicates that the person is not focused on anything in particular. That is the look often referred to as 'glazed.'

Auditory Responsiveness

- **Eyes looking towards the right:** When a person's eyes shift straight towards the right, it means the person is in the process of constructing a sound.
- **Eyes looking towards the left:** When a person's eyes shift straight towards the left, it indicates that the person recalls a sound.

Audio-Digital Responsiveness

- **Eyes looking downward, then switching to the left:** When someone drops their eyes and then proceeds to turn

their eyes to the left, this signals that the person is engaged in internal dialogue.
- **Eyes looking right down then left to right:** When a person looks down and then proceeds to turn their eyes to the left and then to the right in consecutive movements, it means the person is engaged in negative self-talk.

Kinesthetic Responsiveness

Here, the person looks directly down, only to turn the eyes to the right. That is an indication that the person is evaluating emotional status. It further indicates that the person is not at ease:

- Verbal responses

- Rhythmic speech

The idea here is not to be poetic as you speak, but to speak at a regular pace. The recommended pace of speaking is equated to the heartbeat, say, between 45 and 72 beats per minute. At that pace, you are likely to sustain the listener's attention and establish greater receptivity to what you're saying. While normal conversational speed averages about 140 words per minute, slowing down a little and taking time to pause is highly effective to sustain people's attention. Your regular cadence should be punctuated by fluctuations in tone and emphasis in order not to sound monotonous.

Repeating Key Words

When you try to influence someone, some keywords or phrases carry additional weight as far as your message is concerned. This speaking method is a way of embedding the message in the listener and subtly suggesting that your message is valid and worthy of reception. Repeating key words also suggests commitment, conviction, and mastery of the subject matter.

Using Strongly Suggestive Language

Use a supportive and positive language of what you are saying, using a selection set of strong, descriptive words or phrases. As you do this, you should observe the person you are speaking to closely, in a way that makes them feel as though you see right through them and aware of what they are thinking.

Don't be invasive about this or aggressive. Merely suggest that you have a keen appreciation of what makes people tick by way of your gaze. It places you in a dominant position, especially when accompanied by dominant body language, like "steepling." It helps to use suitable, complementary body language as you speak to underscore the message subtly.

Touching the Person Lightly, As You Speak

Touching the person as you speak to them draws their attention to you in a relaxed and familiar way. By employing this technique, you're preparing the listener to absorb what you say to them, a way of programming attentiveness. Those engaging in inter-gender conversations in the workplace should take great care with this technique, as it can lead to misunderstandings.

Using a Mixture of "Hot" and "Vague" Words

"Hot" words are those that tend to provoke specific sensations in the listener. When you use them to influence someone's thinking, it is advisable to use them in a suitable pattern. Examples of phrases containing hot words are: it means; feel free; see this; because; hear this. The effect of employing these words and phrases is that you're directing influencing the listener's state of mind, including how that person feels, imagines, and perceives.

You're also appealing to the sense most prevalent in the listener's perceptive style (as observed through the movement of their eyes). For example, the phrase "hear this" will appeal to those who indicate a tendency to respond most actively to auditory stimuli.

Using the Interspersal Technique

The interspersal technique states one thing while hoping to impress on the listener something entirely different. For example, you could make a positive statement like:

"John is very generous, but some people take advantage of him and treat him as gullible."

When someone hears this statement, the likely assumption is that you want people to appreciate John's generosity. That is likely to be the message heard, and yet, the subtext is that while John is generous, he is also considered gullible and, thus, at a disadvantage in life when it comes to other people. Your hidden agenda may influence the listener to think of John as gullible, which calls into question his judgment. So, emphasize the words "but" and "gullible."

The word "but" serves to transition the perceived compliment to John to an implicit slight. The techniques just described form strategies in the service of influencing people.

They're not intended to force a viewpoint or to control people's behavior for nefarious ends. These techniques are intended to modify undesirable behaviors, resulting in workplace difficulties, including staff failure to work well together or complete team projects.

They're also accommodating in relationships with young people and children, whether at home or in a learning environment.

Techniques of subtle manipulative effects like those described, though capable of influencing people and their behavior, don't amount to anything even approaching coercion. The person being spoken to chooses all responses and is merely influenced or steered toward those responses.

Chapter 12. Protecting Yourself From NLP Mind Control

Now we get how the whole thing works, we're not that fond of it, but we understand the basics. The main question now, though, is how do you guard against it? That's really what we've been trying to figure out this whole time. How do you prevent someone from pulling all that NLP mumbo jumbo on you when you're not looking? This part of the guide is for you because we have a few pointers for you.

Beware of Matchers

The first thing you're going to want to do is to take in and apply everything you've just learned. Remember all that stuff about matching and mirroring? Well, now you need to be on the lookout for it. When you speak to someone you think is trying to control you, make a point to note how they react to your body language. Are they sitting in the same pattern you are? Are they copying your movements as well?

If you're unsure, try testing it out by changing your posture and then wait to see if they mimic it. With pro NLP practitioners, the mimicking may be a bit subtler and a bit more delayed, but the unskilled ones are a total giveaway. They'll copy the posture right away, and automatically, you know what you're up against.

Now that you know, you can either call them out on their behavior or, if you want to have a little fun, start applying NLP on them to confuse them! Not only will you catch them off guard, but if you can pull it off, you can get them to tell you what their whole ploy was all about and who put them up to it. Total win!

Consciously Infuse Randomness in Your Eye Movement

When it comes to confusing your opponent and playing them at their own game, there is little going to give you the same amount of satisfaction as random play. Random eye movements are like going to the gym with your iPod on shuffle. Nobody knows what's coming on after. It's basically like trolling your manipulators in real-time, and it can be quite fun.

Any NLP user worth their salt is going to go in hard with the whole eye movement thing. It is because your eye movements tell them how you assess and store information, which is precisely why some people can tell if you are lying or cheating just by looking at your eyes. When they say your eyes speak volumes, this is what they mean!

So how do you avoid being read by an NLP practitioner? Simple, use random eye movements. As you are speaking, make a point to look left or right or up or down. You can even make a game of it. Left for complex sentences, down for every question, and simple sentences can go right or up, depending on whether they start with a vowel.

Pick Up on Ambiguity

One of the tricks that NLP kind of sneaks in from hypnotherapy is the full use of vague, unclear language. A great example of the use of this technique is Donald Trump's "Make America Great" Again Campaign.

Even though the now-president went around campaigning about making a better version of America, he never really broke down what that meant. It was such a hazy term that it could mean anything to anyone, and that was precisely what he wanted.

Whenever anyone starts using stuff like that on you, such as "release your inner troubles and feel the world move slowly around you in conjunction with your prospective earthly successes." What you're doing is allowing hypnotherapy to program your internal state in a specific form. It helps the other person when they then try to convince you to do something that benefits them.

Anytime you feel that someone is trying to do something like that to you, force yourself to snap out of it and ask specific questions, "What exactly do you mean by 'great'?" or "What potential are you talking about?" Take note; all you have to do is point it out. Once you've done that, you're home free!

Be Hypersensitive to People Permitting You to Do Stuff

The other thing you should watch out for? Permissive language. When a person says something like "you can do XYZ" or "Feel free to make yourself at home" or even something tempting like, "If you want, you can borrow the new Avengers movie from me," what they are doing is preparing you to enter into a trance state. You see, experienced NLP users never outright tell their subjects to do anything. They suggest, recommend, or allow. In this way, the subject feels like they are in control, whereas control was wiped out a long time ago in reality! So then, feel free to say no thanks!

Read Between the Lines

We're onto reading between the lines. You have to keep in mind that people who use or people who are using NLP to control you or to manipulate you tend to use specific controlled langue, and nine out of ten times, you are not going to know what hit you.

How do they do it? Double meanings. And you'll find them in the unexpected places, so skilled NLP users who are good at what they do know how to use double meaning infused sentences to get you to think the way they want you to. Imagine that you are the evil witch's neighbor from the Hansel and Gretel story; now you don't eat kids, but you do have a thing for snacks. Your NLP user, A.K.A "the evil witch" comes up to you and says, "Children make nutritious snacks, just in case you were wondering." Sure the witch claims she was talking about their production capacity, but what you heard and processed was something a little different, and already you're a bit more inclined to take a little nibble.

Be Attentive

You need to be very careful about how much attention you are paying to your surroundings and what's going on in them. We get you that you can't always be super alert, but you need to know that you are vulnerable when you aren't alert. For example, an essential tactic that employers use when negotiating salary packages is waiting until the employee in question seems a little off and then jumping in. Saying that they haven't negotiated a pay difference for Tom, Dick, and Harry and don't foresee a lot of change in the other employees. Not much change at all, they repeat. Automatically, now that you are asked how much change in salary you expect, you say not much change—congratulations! You've just been programmed!

Watch Your Mouth

Another important tip? Watch what you say. Master manipulators tend to create a false sense of urgency to make you feel that you have to do this particular thing by this specific time, or else something drastic will happen. You don't have a choice. You have to do this now! What do you do? Well, nothing. Yes, seriously, nothing. Never make any important decisions at the drop of a hat. Chances are you're not the president of the United States, meaning no nuclear codes lie with you, which of course, means that you don't need to make any immediate decisions without consulting people. You don't have to make any quick decisions at all.

Sit tight. Getting you to commit is a classic dark psychology move to create a sense of obligation after being exploited. Please don't fall for it!

Trust Your Gut

And your final rule, which also happens to be your most important, is to trust your gut. Your instincts know a lot more than you do, mostly because your subconscious mind is processing signs and symbols at a rate your conscious brain can't even begin to fathom. So if it is out there telling you that something is up and that something needs to be done about it, then you need to make sure that you are on your guard ready to get things done because, like a used car salesman, you are more likely than not in the hands of a master practitioner.

Chapter 13. Smart and Wise Goal-Setting Using Neuro-Linguistics

NLP or Neuro-Linguistic Programming explores how you think and feel. It examines the inner language that you usually use to represent your life experiences. It studies human interaction and achievement and uses this knowledge to help you achieve excellence in all aspects of your life.

The concepts behind NLP techniques are based on the fact that you already have the necessary internal resources and capabilities to effectively change your life and the lives of the people around you. NLP helps you in your goal setting and in taking the necessary actions to realize your goal.

Easy NLP Techniques to Help You Achieve Your Goals

Be Specific About the Things That You Want

It repeatedly reiterates what has been echoed: you must have a clear understanding of what it is that you exactly want. You need to have a noticeable or clear vision of what you are aiming for. Look at it this way; imagine you are sailing in the middle of the ocean. Without a clear vision of where you want to go and just going with the flow and where the water will take you, you will fail. If you are blindly going through life, how do you expect to get to where you want to go?

Ask Yourself What You Want

NLP recommends asking questions like: "If I continue doing the things I am doing now, where will I be a year from now?" "Am I happy where I am now and the direction I am going?" "If I am not happy, what should I do instead? What would make me happy?" When you can answer similar questions, it will be easier to identify what you want.

Create Mental Images of Your Goals

The moment you have established what you want to achieve, put them into writing. If buying your dream house, create images of the actual house, including the smallest details as design, location, and neighborhood. You must create powerful internal images and play them on your mind over and over. Be realistic and think about actual colors, what you see around, the smell of the flowers, or the sound of your neighbor's dog barking in the background. Create a "movie" in your mind. Go as far as seeing what you are wearing on that particular day that you are finally buying the house. Make the movie as detailed as possible, as if it is happening. It is bringing visualization techniques to a higher level.

Write Your Goals As If They Are Already Being Realized and Focus on Them

You might find it helpful to use words in the present tense and then create the images. You'll create a more powerful impact if you picture your goal like it is happening right this very moment. Keep in mind that NLP teaches you and allows you to move towards the things you intently focus on. By doing so, you are attracting success. This technique will enable you to influence what the universe gives you. You must maintain your focus on a clear positive image of what you want you to achieve, in this case, buying your dream house. Throughout your journey towards attaining your goal, you have to maintain your focus on that goal.

Use Your Goal As Your Motivation to Keep on Moving Toward It

Think of action items that will bring you closer to your goal. Devise plans of action on how you can continue to move forward. Imagine that you are already there at the "finish line" and look back at how you were able to get there. It might help if you imagine a physical mind with several essential points. It is the path that you have to take to reach the realization of your goal. There may be obstacles, but if you keep your focus on the result, you'll think of ways to overcome those obstacles and continue with your journey. Having a clear picture of the things you have to do to reach your goal helps you achieve it.

Look for a Role Model

Look for a person you can look up to and learn from. Read their success stories. Take pointers from them or if you cannot reach them, find resources that speak about them. Most stories of famous and successful people contain tips and guidelines on how they attained their current stature. Watch video clips, testimonies, and books about them. Learn from their life lessons and mistakes.

Act!

You have the goals, and you have established what you want to do, but you'll never achieve anything if you don't begin to act. Nothing and no one can achieve your goals for you, you have to act, and it is the first step you have to take. Act to begin moving towards the fulfillment of your goals. If you want to buy a house, start saving or considering taking on additional income sources. One small step is actually what you need to get you going.

Plan!

Once you have acted on your goal, you have to make sure that you have a concrete plan to achieve your goal. You have to have a timescale. As you move towards attaining your goal, continue to stay focused, and create positive images of the final goal in your mind.

Exude Positivity

Having confidence doesn't mean you won't fail. It means that while you might encounter challenges, you remain confident to push forward. You might commit a misstep, but if you use that as an opportunity to learn, then you'll get back on track.

Be Flexible

Things do not turn out the way you want to, even if you work hard at it. You need to keep on going, move forward, and try other options.

Keep on Going

You might fail along the way, and you might encounter rejection, but that shouldn't discourage you from continuing to follow your dreams. Keep on moving forward.

Chapter 14. Introduction of Persuasion

Persuasion is the ability to transmit ideas and disseminate them by those who act as recipients. It translates more effectively as the ability that human beings have through a relationship, to convince others. Persuasion is a tool that can be used in fields such as marketing, advertising, and commerce, basically sectors of the economy in which the public is sensitive to various interactions with environmental media and where the decision is the objective of who persuades.

How Does it Work?

Let us elaborate on a scene in which a seller wants his products to be acquired by the buyers; besides being useful, they must be attractive and, in one way or another, more desirable than that of the competition. It is achieved with persuasion, which attracts clients by offering the best product or service attributes, effectively providing comfort to the buyer by relating the most promotional aspects to the most personal. In turn, persuasion generates competition and demand in the market, generating dynamism of intentions and offers that fosters sustainable economies.

Another use of persuasion that we see in a society continually is in the application of the law. In a trial, the lawyers, using the law as the main tool, use the elements in their favor and persuade the jury and the judge that they are valid to win the case.

We are always waiting for others who live in our environment to reproduce or share our ideas; even unintentionally, people seek to persuade others to fulfill their ends. A wife who asks her husband to optimize expenses is trying to convince him that it is the best for both. Either way, each person's ideas will be interpreted as an intention for others to apply and build their ideas based on the initial idea. Persuasion can be so extreme that they can change the way a person thinks. It all depends on what the person who persuades another looks for.

Psychological Tricks to Increase Your Persuasive Power

Evaluate Context and Time

The foundation for increasing your power of persuasion is context and the exact time. The first requirement sets a standard for what is acceptable and can be done, while the right timing makes your chances increase or decrease considerably. Trying to persuade your boss to raise you well when he is nervous or talking about an important issue is not a timely approach. Therefore, having this notion of timing is critical in the persuasion process.

Remember That Persuasion Is Different from Manipulation

To manipulate is to coerce someone into doing something that is not in their best interest. However, persuasion is the art of persuading people to do something that is in their interest and benefits you.

Speak What People Want to Hear

You will not be able to persuade someone who has no interest in what you are saying. Generally, people are interested in themselves and spend most of their time thinking about money, love, or health. Therefore, to increase your persuasion power, it is necessary to learn to talk to people about themselves consistently. Remember: If you show interest in what they want and say, you will always have your attention.

Be Persistent

Have you noticed that historical figures who persuaded large masses achieved this with much persistence in their messages? If you focus on demonstrating value and staying focused, you are much more likely to get what you want.

Greet People Sincerely

We are all affected by compliments, whether we like it or not. And people tend to believe more in someone who gives them good feelings. So greet people when they deserve it, highlight their qualities and achievements. You will see how, practically and honestly, you will be able to persuade someone more easily. Investing in reciprocity is also very effective in this process; after all, when you do something for someone, that person feels compelled to do something for you too. It is part of the evolution of our DNA.

Create a Sense of Urgency

To increase your persuasive power, you need to create a sense of urgency in people by making them want something or act right now. If you're not motivated enough to want something right now, you probably won't like it in the future. Therefore, invest in your power of persuasion in the present, betting on the urgency of things.

Value the Images

Remember: what we see is more important than what we hear. Therefore, hone your first impressions to increase your persuasive power by increasing your ability to paint an image of experience you can offer others in the future.

Be Flexible and Communicate Simply

Have you noticed how flexible children are in their behaviors? They do everything, in every means they can to get what they want from their parents, and most of the time, they can. Therefore, adopting a rigid posture is never a good way to increase your persuasive power. Communicating is also another important point because the art of persuasion is to simplify something so that it is quick and straightforward to understand.

Chapter 15. History of Persuasion

The persuasion can be traced back to Greek origins. It was used as a tool by great orators to get their message across to the common folk. For a country that has created the political frameworks behind democracy, persuasion was immensity popular. If you have ever taken an advanced writing class that went over rhetorical analysis, you might recognize the three rhetorical modes of pathos, ethos, and logos. Aristotle billed these as the three main appeals that an orator could make to move their audience.

Its usage implies that the audience is a malleable entity, like putty. A skilled orator's words can manipulate the audience like a child might manipulate a piece of putty. Other times, persuasion is used to rile up an already popular cause, to begin with, but that had been up to that point undisclosed.

The three rhetorical modes are important because they represent three different attack vectors that a manipulator might use to persuade their audience. Again, any form of persuasion is a type of mental manipulation, but it doesn't become a psychological attack until it becomes malicious. In other words, there is a difference between plain old persuasive arguments and using persuasion to carry out dark psychology.

Regular persuasion is the type that might make you vote for a candidate or buy some product (though some would argue that modern-day advertising has dark psychology aspects). On the other hand, malicious persuasion might entice you to go against your set of morals and beliefs. This sort of persuasion is dangerous because an attacker's arguments may seem very convincing to you when, in reality, they are just cleverly designed to trick you. At the same time, the persuasion is being used to benefit someone else.

The dark psychology mindset tells us that there are people out there with less than kind objectives. They may be after your wealth, your emotional labor, your body, your mind, or just a few minutes of your attention. And all of this is theoretically possible through the levying of persuasive techniques. But first, we should talk about everyday persuasion in the traditional sense.

Modern-Day Aristotle

No matter what persuasive argument you come across, they will have all of the semblances of Aristotle's appeals, mixed in with a modern "secret sauce" that is unique to the persuader (and indeed the situation). It is still worth talking about persuasion and persuasive arguments because they are the cornerstone of all manipulation types. If a manipulator were a boxer, persuasion techniques would be like their left jab. Not as powerful as a KO punch, but still the punch that lands them the most points and slows down their opponent.

A modern-day Aristotle can be anyone. A politician, a used car salesman, even your mother is trying to convince you to move closer to home. All of these would be Aristotle's have something in common: they want something from you. And it is your job to decide whether their needs are genuine and desirable for all parties. They will no doubt stop at anything to convince you that they are. To do this, you have to separate their argument from the chaff. For persuasive techniques, the chaff is usually the bubbly language or the sharp edge in their arguments that cut you into you.

But beware. Just because it cuts you, it doesn't mean that it is deep or meaningful to you in any way. Many skillful persuaders will only pander to already preconceived notions that their audiences may have. They say something that they know their audience will like and instantly become that much more credible.

But someone trying to come up with a novel argument will first have to design a rhetorical strategy using any of the three rhetorical modes available. It is true whether they are trying to form an essay, a speech, or persuade you into doing something. The world of sales is chock-full of strategies used designed to get you to buy. A competent salesperson may try to get to know you first (especially if the purchase is large, like a new house or car). They wish to form a relationship on a first-name basis and then pose as a close friend.

In the world of sales, the only thing that matters is the purchase. If a client decides to buy, then whatever strategies used to make that sale are fair game. It opens the ground for deploying several different types of psychological tricks against the unsuspecting client. For example, a salesperson may introduce them to a high-end item that is purposely out of their buying range and then redirect them towards an item of similar functionality perceived as being more affordable.

A family looking to buy a new laptop for their college-bound son may be directed towards the expensive and latest Apple laptop product only to realize that it is well out of their budget. The savvy salesperson can then walk them to the Windows computers aisle and show them an alternative product that is the same color as an Apple computer but has a different operating system and is slightly less performative. Now, that other laptop may still be a flagship item and have a sizable price tag, but it is perceived as a good buy by the family because the salesperson showed them an item they believe to be state of the art.

Such tricks are less persuasive strategies than they are crude psychological manipulation. More psychological persuasion involves more trickery and deception—the type of things one would expect except dark psychology techniques. Indeed, the salesman trick of going high and then going low can pass as a type of emotional manipulation. It is subtle, but there is clear pandering towards what a client believes their money can buy them. First, they are shown what is considered to be the "it" product. But since they can't afford it, the salesman puts them on an emotional roller coaster of desire.

In a way, it is a projection of what the client believes they deserve. Sure, they can't afford the best, but since they feel like they deserve the best (and since the salesman believes they deserve the best), buying the other best product is an easy choice. And if they can afford the high-end object the salesman shows them first, their job is already finished. In other words, whether the client buys the expensive item or the lesser expensive one, the salesman still wins. It is a perfect example of a psychological manipulation that is difficult to detect in the moment's heat and has a high success rate.

Chapter 16. Six Principles of Persuasion

To learn and enhance the art of persuasion, you need to be aware of the underlying principles that will enable you to harness your influence. Generally, Human beings are a touchy lot; one wrong move and you're going to lose all ability to persuade people to join your team. You need to make critical decisions that are guided by the necessary fundamental principles. Reciprocity, consistency, social evidence, liking, authority, and scarcity are the six principles of persuasion.

Reciprocity Principle

Reciprocity does to others as you would have them do to you. Reciprocity calls for respect and kindness as you go about your everyday experiences. It's a good thing to show kindness to others that makes others feel better about your interaction. Besides that, your way of earning chips that you can cash in after is to do well. If you have been very nice and kind to someone else, you have a better chance that they will be nice and kind to you.

If you are hoping to persuade a person, you must decently behave towards them. Speak a word of kindness, give them a favor, or even buy them a gift. They will be more agreeable after when you need to convince them to do something. After all, you have proved yourself to be a kind human being who cares for him.

The Cohesion Principle

Consistency in persuasion works this way: once you have convinced them to agree to smaller ones, people are more likely to commit to bigger tasks or favors. That is, if you get them to spring a puddle for you, you can get someone to swim oceans for you. A few studies have been done to support this hypothesis. For example, in one study, a group of researchers asked some homeowners to put up a hideous Drive Safely billboard on their front lawn. Very few homeowners declared yes. However, the researchers had to take a different approach to the experiment: first, they got homeowners to agree to the small commitment to putting up a Drive Safely postcard in their home's front windows. Ten days after, they returned with the request for a billboard. This time, despite its lack of aesthetic appeal, more homeowners agreed to put up the billboard. The reason for this is that the homeowners subconsciously felt compelled to keep up with their earlier reaction.

The technique of foot-in-the-door compliance is premised on consistency. It means getting people to consent to a bigger request by first using smaller requests to check the waters. If you want to execute this strategy cleverly, your target will need to be trained to be consistent with their responses to your question.

The Liking Principle

If some people like you, they're more likely to fulfill your demands, no matter what that may be. A person who is unlike and who is also unlikeable will hear no more times than a well-liked person. But how is it that you get people to like you? The secret to being loved is a combination of three main factors, according to science. First of all, people prefer the ones close to them. You must find common ground with them to look close to the person you are trying to convince. For example, many foreigners have learned that learning and speaking the local language is the simplest way to become more likable. You also need and practice to be mindful of is flattery while making yourself more likable. If you are using it well, flattery will open many doors for you.

Citizens prefer those paying attention to them. If you want to ask someone to do something for you, start by offering them a genuine compliment first. Just because this is called flattery doesn't mean you need to be effusive about it. Too excessive in your praise will be counterproductive to your need to be liked. Last but not least, be the kind of person that is usually pleasant and cooperative in achieving mutual goals, and you will be one step closer to being pleasant. If you're always stepping on the toes of others to get what you want, you'll have very few friends, and this won't help your case when you need to convince someone in the future. Remember, being pleasant and cooperative doesn't imply being a doormat. Sometimes, it merely means putting some little effort into helping a person achieve a vital goal. For example, if a colleague struggles with a due report, offer to help them with the printing and mailing process. It's not a lot of work, but you're going to go from an uninvolved, unwritten colleague to a kind and helpful colleague. You can cash this chip after if you wish.

The Authority Theory

Compared to a complete newbie, a person who is an authority figure in a particular field will have an easier time influencing others. If you want to persuade or influence more people to do something specific, you need to build your credibility by making yourself seem like you have expertise in whatever field you play. This principle is a key reason why professionals in their field display their diplomas. Think about it—when, for example, you step into a therapist's office, you would probably deliberately look out for the sort of qualifications they have hanging on their walls. If your therapist has many credentials displayed in this way, you will probably feel a sense of comfort in their expertise and experience. As such, you'll quickly accept and follow any advice they have for you. Essentially the therapist has managed to influence you without even saying a word.

It's a fact that if you're the only one talking about it, your authority won't be taken very seriously. As such, you have to make sure, so to speak, that you recruit others to beat the drums on your behalf. Subtle ways exist to do this. You can identify a field in the office you are passionate about and become that field's office guru. It could be Microsoft Excel or Reporting for some people. The guy known as the Excel office guru will have a much easier time getting things out of people because they already know he knows what he's talking about. He has also proved to be likable and helpful by solving all of their problems with Excel, and his colleagues may want to pay him back in some way. You don't need to learn Excel to make your mark around the world.

Scarcity Principle

The laws of supply and demand are easy and straightforward in economics: when supply is low and demand is high, prices rise. To translate this, the value of scarcity builds. If you are a business person who wants to persuade people to purchase your product or service, it highlights that the product is on offer for only a limited time. Furthermore, let the clients know that they will lose significantly if they do not access this product on time. If the marketing message is packaged in this way, more people will be rushing to beat the time limit on your product.

It is essential to become a scarce product yourself in the business and personal relations world. If you're not there for others whenever they need you, you'll quickly lose your worth. If you want to remain your aura of mystery and power around you, you must learn the art of being inaccessible and unavailable. When you appear, your word will be respected more than a person's word that continuously appears and speaks out of all importance and meaning.

The Consensus Theory

People look at others similar to them in everyday interactions for clues about what to do or say. An individual who is a good influencer knows that buying into their idea is all it takes is one individual, and the whole crowd does. There are different ways you can apply the consensus principle to your benefit. For example, in an office setting, you can get a part of the staff to agree to a cause and champion that causes their colleagues to do so. These colleagues are more likely to be convinced of the worthy cause because their peers have said so.

For example, if you've ever purchased anything from Amazon, you might have seen that it includes a part showing the other items purchased by clients who ordered the product you just purchased. How does that segment affect you as a buyer? More often than not, you'll probably consider buying those other items because they were bought by these clients who have similar tastes and needs to yours. Initially, you may not have planned to buy the additional items, but just the fact that others did it will make you think you also need to. That is, in effect, the principle of consensus.

Chapter 17. Theories on Persuasion

There are a few different theories on persuasion that we should start to understand. Before we talk about these, let's take a more in-depth look at what processes persuasion might be done through. How can we completely change the way we are thinking or feeling based on another person's ability to alter our feelings? There are a few core elements to what persuasion is and what you can use to define this process.

Persuasion is when a message is transferred from one person to the other. This message might be a way of life, such as religion. Have you ever seen signs of someone wanting to share their religion with you? Maybe they have passed free information like brochures or mini booklets to get you on their side. It is an example of how others might try to convince you of their messages. They will be using symbols and words to try and get you to understand where they are coming from. Some will go as far as to scare you as well, making you think that something bad might happen to you if you choose not to follow what they're stating. Persuasion goes as far back as human history does. Some methods of persuasion have been natural in our society. There are other times when persuasion has been a little more forced. Perhaps it is a physical skill ingrained in the anatomy that we use to help us survive. It could simply be a survival tactic or deeply ingrained in our society and the language we use.

Persuasion is always going to be more positive when you can give the other person their freedom to choose. When you take that freedom away and become more forceful, this can turn into manipulation, brainwashing, and other dark psychology methods. We will break all three of these down for you to better recognize the different levels of persuasive behavior. First, let's start to talk about some other theories about how and why persuasion can be so effective.

The first one is conditioning theory. It explains how prolonged exposure could be "conditioning" us to fall more efficiently for a message. It is something easily seen on the level of advertisements. Think of a brand, specifically maybe a candy brand that you like. Whatever this is, recall the last time you saw an advertisement for it. They will use signs of the actual product and what this might look like. In a commercial, they might show someone eating it with the same branded colors in the background. Maybe they have a simple phrase or logo that you remember immediately without even trying. Then, you make your way to a grocery store and see this same product with the same colors and are more inclined to purchase this because you have already been conditioned to do so. If you had never seen an advertisement for the product, you might not notice the display of candy sitting there when you walk in the store, but they have already planted this idea in your head, so you're way more willing actually to purchase this.

The other theory that we have is the cognitive dissonance theory. It states how we will always be looking for ways to connect our thoughts and behaviors with reality. Even if you have thoughts different from what you do, your brain will look for ways to justify this kind of behavior. For example, let's say that you are overweight, and you don't want to be. You'd love it if you could lose thirty pounds. However, you continue to eat unhealthy junk food and skip the gym every day. Your actions are not aligning with your beliefs, and this creates cognitive dissonance. It is essential because it will show how your brain can be persuaded easily even when you know certain information isn't true. Your brain wants your actions to match your beliefs, so it will convince you to do one of two things. You can either find that motivation to go to the gym and eat healthier and then your actions match your beliefs of wanting to lose weight. Alternatively, your mind might instead convince you that there is nothing wrong with being unhealthy. You might assure yourself that what you are told about your health is all a lie, or maybe that you don't deserve even to have a healthy body. Whatever it is, your brain is going to try and fill in those blanks and make you believe something that isn't entirely true, all so that your actions align with your belief. It is something that might end up hurting others in the long run. Think of a crazy cult leader. They will have things that they believe, and after a while, it might not be just enough for them to be the only ones to believe this. Instead of changing their mind about their beliefs, they might try to convince others to believe the same thing in an attempt to validate their perspective. It can be toxic and damaging behavior, but it is something that our brain might naturally do.

These theories are essential to understand because they will start to give you a little insight into how or why someone might be trying to convince themselves or others of their message. We will talk about the basic persuasion techniques that people use soon, but we must first understand the motive. If you can't discover a motive behind someone's persuasion, then they might not necessarily be trying to be manipulative, intentionally or not. Always ask, "Why are they doing this?" whenever you might be questioning someone's goal for whether or not they are manipulative.

Chapter 18. Persuasion Techniques

Persuasion techniques also have their level. Whether you are a beginner, an intermediate one, or an advanced user of persuasion of techniques, you should be able to discern when to apply these techniques to maximize their effectiveness.

Basic Persuasion Techniques

By Association

It is one persuasion technique commonly used by people who are in the early stage of improving their influencing skills. With this technique, you try to link the particular service, product, or idea with another thing that is already liked by your target audience. Association is a powerful technique, although it does not explicitly claim that you will achieve these things.

Let's take an example—associating the concept of 'family' with the brand such as Coke through emotional transfer has been an effective tool for many years. The term 'victory' has also been associated with another brand, 'Nike.'

By Bandwagon

Another persuasion technique that can be used by newbies is the Bandwagon method. What you want to achieve is to make other people realize that 'everyone else is already doing it, and so should you.' Most people want to have a sense of belonging, and they do not want to be left behind. So, in this technique, your ultimate goal is to make sure that your prospect is ready to hop on the bandwagon with you.

By Testimonials

OK, this is probably one of the most common methods, yet it works well despite being around for decades. It is because people tend to pay extra attention to celebrities. Whether we admit or not, following a celebrity or being a fan is one of the guilty pleasures anyone can have. When big brands use celebrities, famous athletes, and models, it is easier to influence people into trying the same product.

By Using Humor

Many of the ads that we usually remember are because of the humor injected into it. When we see them, we laugh, and we feel good. Thus, it becomes a great persuasion tool. When you associate your product or service with something that makes people 'feel good,' it becomes easier to influence them. It performs or works when it comes to relationships too. When you can be intelligently funny to someone, it becomes a lot easier to influence him or her to continue to like you.

By Repetition

As they say, repetition is the key to retention. To influence and persuade people, you should be able to repeat your message subtly and in various ways. Have you ever experienced humming or singing an ad jingle in your head? You may not like the product itself, but since you see the ad almost every day over the Web, on TV, or even in print ads, something about it sticks. When it sticks, it becomes a lot less complex to influence the person.

By Experts

It is a form of testimonials too. Commonly, people would look at the logical reasoning or expert claims behind a particular item. If you are an expert in one area, it would be easier to find an expert testimonial. For instance, if your prospective clients are parents or moms—then the expert should be a mom as well who is known in a particular field.

By Bribery

Yes, we all love freebies, don't we? It is one technique you can employ, as well. When you want to influence people, give them more than they expect—discount, promo, holidays, etc. Influencing people also means giving them good value for money, good returns on their investments, etc. As you hone your skills, you will then influence more effectively using the succeeding techniques.

Intermediate Persuasion Techniques

By Being Charismatic

For instance, if you present yourself to be bold, confident, strong, and sleek, you could expect people to listen to you more. Like, if you get persuaded into buying something if the endorser itself is someone that tickles your fancy.

By Presenting Novel Ideas

People love new things. It is no longer surprising that people place great faith in technological advancements. One method to influence people is by presenting an idea that is new to them. Giving something novel gives them that sense of pride in being one of the first to get it.

By Using Rhetorical Questions

One of the most useful or effective ways to elicit reactions from people is by asking them questions. Questions such as, "Do you want to become a millionaire before you hit 30?" "Do you want to live debt-free?" "Do you want to be as stunning as Monica Bellucci?"—these are all set up to build alignment and to establish rapport before the sales pitch takes over. Usually, these are the type of questions that would capture the attention so that your prospect would stay longer and listen to the sales pitch.

By Nostalgia

It is the opposite method of #9 By Presenting Novel Ideas. In this method, you try to influence people by making them excited about the 'good old days.' As changes come rapidly, some people get tired of it and want to get back to the days when life is simpler. A good example is the revival of the Nokia 3310 in this time of advanced smartphones or that easy-to-prepare food that brings back childhood memories.

By Offering Simple Solutions

We live in a complicated or complex world, and people are continually seeking simpler solutions. If you intend to influence someone or a target market, offer relief by proposing a simple solution to any problem. For instance, advertisers like the concept of 'one-stop-shop' for any particular service, enabling consumers to address their multiple needs in one place.

By Showing Slippery Slope

It is quite similar to using 'fear' as a weapon for influence. Instead of predicting positive results, you can influence people by showing them the looming dangers of not acting and deciding immediately. For instance, to influence and persuade people to invest, you could show the possible scenarios when the recession kicks in. Anything that could give them a picture of what could happen if they do not do something can be used in this technique.

By Presenting Scientific Evidence

In this method, you get to present facts that would eventually influence someone to decide instantly. Many people tend to consider themselves 'people of Science,' or those keen on knowing one product's scientific principle before buying them. For case, if you are trying to sell a collagen-based skincare product, you need to explain the role of collagen and what it does in the biological makeup of the skin. By showing pretty girls using it in ads may not be sufficient.

You will learn the techniques that influencers of the advanced level users. Note that you do not have to jump to this list right away. You can utilize any from the recent list to know which suits your style best.

Advanced Persuasion Techniques

By Analogy

A good analogy helps in influencing people and creates a sense of truthfulness, which helps establish your credibility. A weak analogy, on the other hand, can instantly break interest. When using this method, make sure the comparison is still logical and not over the top.

By Understanding Group Dynamics

It is a more intense version of the 'Bandwagon' technique. Understanding the specific beliefs of a group of people will help understand the influence method to use. For occasion, if you are selling a high-end product, you would certainly look for a market that can afford them. However, you can also capture the market that aspires to be part of the group.

Ad Hominem

It is a Latin phrase that means 'against the man.' In this technique, you do not influence people by attacking a product, but the maker itself. This method is also referred to as 'attacking the messenger.' It takes skills and a colossal amount of research to do this. Incorrect use of this method may lead to other complex problems, so use this with care and discretion.

By Scapegoating Method

It is one powerful method that politicians of today make use of influence voters. They tend to highlight the failures of former politicians or leaders to capture the trust of the voters. Another example is when they blame a particular person, organization, or race for a problem.

One clear example here is when politicians vying for a position in an incoming election would blame the undocumented immigrants for the rising unemployment rate. Unemployment itself is a complex matter that is bound by multiple factors.

Knowing the Right Timing

Timing is of the essence even when it comes to influencing. You need to know what is happening around you, current affairs, and current problems that need immediate solutions. For instance, an ill-timed proposal can instantly go up in smoke when people find the timing irrelevant.

Card Stacking

In this method, you do not tell the whole story but only select the parts considered favorable to your audience or target market. While this could work well, it is imperative to know how you could justify the 'hiding' of the facts. Again, as this is a tricky method, you need to be 'great' to make it work.

As you can see, there are 'dirty' tricks that people can do to influence people. While they are entirely incorrect, it takes a great deal of care, courage, and common sense to use them. If you are not exactly comfortable using advanced techniques, you can still use the beginner and intermediate methods.

Remember, each one of us has an influencing style that we are most comfortable with. Evaluate yourself and find your own. If you have finally grasped how you could do better, it's now time to learn how you could increase your influence in this digital era.

Chapter 19. Difference Between Persuasion and Manipulation

Many people fail to recognize the nuances between manipulation and persuasion. Although both seek to convince someone else to do something else, they are quite different in enough key ways to be classified entirely differently. One is only beneficial to the manipulator (manipulation), while the other ideally, should benefit both people. Because of these key differences, manipulation becomes far more insidious than persuasion. The manipulator sees the other person as a tool, a means to an end, whereas the persuader sees the other person as a partner.

Defining Persuasion

Though persuasion involves changing someone else's mind, it is not necessarily a bad thing—there are plenty of ways to use persuasion innocently or benevolently. Persuasion is any method that will actively change the thoughts, emotions, actions, or attitudes of another person toward another person or thing. This change is seen as a persuasion. It can be done inwardly toward oneself by changing one's attitudes or being done to other people.

Usually, persuasion is used as a form of influence—it is everywhere. It is present in ads, politics, schools, professions, and just about everywhere you could think of. If you can think of something, chances are there is some persuasive layer to it somewhere and somehow.

When persuading someone, four key elements must be present. These four elements are:

- Someone who is doing the persuading

- The message or the persuasion

- A target recipient for the persuasion

- A context that the persuasion is received

Each of these four key elements must be present for something to be considered persuasive. Of course, this means that manipulation would fall within the category of persuasion as well.

Defining Manipulation

In psychology, manipulation is a type of influence or persuasion, but unlike regular persuasion, manipulation is covert, deceptive, or underhanded. It means that, unlike regular persuasion, which seeks to be most honest, manipulation is often untrustworthy. The manipulator will have no concern about lying about the situation or attempting to coerce the target into believing something, so long as he gets what he wants.

The manipulator seeks only to serve himself further—he does not care about the target and does not care about hurting the target. The target is seen as little more than collateral damage—a necessary to get the desired results. As such, manipulation tactics are often quite exploitative and almost always meant to be insidious and harmful.

Successful manipulation requires three key concepts to happen. These three are:

- Concealing the intentions and behaviors while remaining friendly upfront

- Understanding the ways the victim or target is vulnerable and using those vulnerabilities to the manipulator's advantage.

- Being ruthless enough to not care about the harm caused to the victim

Manipulation can take several different forms, but most of them follow the covert, harmful, and causing no guilt to the manipulator.

Key Differences

Ultimately, persuasion and manipulation are quite similar: They are both forms of social influence, but that is where the similarities end. While persuasion is generally positive, even within dark psychology, manipulation is not. Manipulation is harmful, ruthless, and insidious in every way, shape, and form.

When you are trying to choose whether something is manipulative or persuasive, there are a few questions you can ask yourself to decide. This simple test can allow you to analyze what you are doing and say to ensure you are making the best choices. If you are not looking to manipulate, but the questions tell you that you are erring on the manipulation side, you know to tone it down slightly, lightening up on the manipulative factors. These questions are:

- What is the intention that has led you to feel the need to convince the other person of something?

- Are you truthful about your intention and the process?

- How does this benefit the other person?

The persuader will be attempting to convince the other person from a good place—they intend to help the other person somehow. While they may benefit too, they are primarily looking out for the other person's best interest. For example, you may try to convince someone to buy a specific car because it will work better for their family than the person currently looking at. It would be seen as persuasion—you are offering facts about the other car and showing how it would likely serve the person longer and better.

On the other hand, the manipulator is not concerned with the other person's needs—the manipulator will attempt to push for whatever benefits them the most. There is no good intention, and there will likely not be much truth either. It is also not likely to benefit the other person in any way and may even be detrimental. For example, the manipulator may try to sell a car that is no good for the buyer simply because the other car may be worth more money and therefore net a much higher commission. The car is not likely to be very good for the buyer's needs, but that is not the manipulator's concern. The manipulator would see that as something the buyer should know on his own and not bother pointing out how the buyer may be making a bad decision, even if the manipulator knows it was wrong.

Chapter 20. Factors That Influence Persuasion

Before you attempt to persuade anyone, some groundwork goes into the process that must be done beforehand. You will not just walk up to a stranger in the street and try to convince that person that they should buy a house or even a piece of paper from you. You have not assessed that person to determine if they need what you are selling or if that person has the means to buy the item. That scenario is farfetched, but the same principle applies to any situation where persuasion is being used.

You need to put thought into how and why you will approach the person or group of people you would like to persuade. The first factor that needs to be assessed is how easily this person or group can be persuaded. You need to know how much work needs to be placed into making the individual(s) see things in the way you do.

The first factor that determines how easy and straightforward it will be to influence other people is whether you are part of their group. Groups can mean several things. Groups can mean family, workplace, gym, or even a social media group. Being part of the group you would like to persuade does the job that much easier because you are seen as one of them. That relatability makes you more trusted. You also have insider knowledge of what makes the group tick. You know their views on particular matters and are less likely to step on toes when implementing the art of persuasion.

Certain qualities make certain people easier to persuade compared to other people. A person's mental health is one of those qualities. Persons who suffer from depression and other mental health issues are more easily swayed to see things from someone else. It is largely because this person is likely to be lacking in aggression and has low self-esteem, both qualities that also make a person more easily persuaded. It is a point that can tip the scale in any direction, though, as a person with a mental health issue might agree with you to avoid the conflict if they do not but are not convinced or persuaded to your point of view.

As it relates to a lack of aggression, people who are typically not prone to showing aggressive tendencies are more agreeable and less likely to challenge the point you bring across to them. People with low self-esteem do not hold themselves or their abilities in high regard. Therefore, they value the opinion of other people more than their own. As a result, they are typically easier to persuade. Slouching posture and the confidence in a person's tone as they speak are indicators of self-esteem levels. If a person is upright and open in their body posture and speaks with high confidence, this person likely has high self-esteem, while the opposite is true for low self-esteem.

People who are socially inept as also easier to convince compared to social butterflies. People who are impaired when it comes to social interactions typically place the burden of the conversation on other people and are less likely to express their opinions freely. This increases the chances that they can be persuaded without challenging the person who is persuading them.

Once you have determined why a particular individual or group needs to be approached for persuasion, you need to figure out how you will cross that bridge to start the process of persuasion naturally. Coming across as awkward or unsure will immediately put your target's guard up, hence making it less likely that you will sway them to your point of view.

If you are not part of the group that you would like to persuade, you need to get the right introduction into that group. Walking or calling will likely not work as we are naturally suspecting people we do not know. This person does not know you or what you stand for and, therefore, will not trust what you have to say. It is why salespeople who cold-call have so much trouble getting a foot in to make the sale. The potential client does not know or trust the salesperson.

Getting someone that the target already knows and trusts is better for forming that bridge. People tend to think that the connections of the people they already know and trust are likely trustworthy because people tend to form connections with people who hold similar views and beliefs.

Sometimes though, it is not possible to get an introduction through a mutual connection. Therefore, as a persuader, you need to be still able to finesse your way into building that connection with the intended target from scratch. Even though cold calling is a sales strategy that many salespeople hate participating in, many salespeople find great success with the technique because they have mastered making the potential client or client comfortable in their company and, further, trusting the message delivery. This mastery comes from having great listening and communication skills.

The first thing that effective listening does is to allow the persuader to observe the target's language. Language, in this instance, refers to the jargon that the target understands or recognizes as applicable. A computer salesperson will have to learn a particular language that includes memory capacity, hard drive space, and monitor resolution. He cannot hope to sell anything to a computer fanatic if he does not understand these terms and others related to computers.

A master persuader knows how to ask questions that allow him or her to gather information about the one to be persuaded and then listens effectively to gain pieces of information that can make it easier to persuade the target. For example, a door to door salesman can walk up to your door to make a sale. However, if he wants to have an effective campaign, he will not just start selling to you. Even if you want or need the product or service that he is selling, you will be wary of this stranger who has come up to your door and is not very trusting of what he has to say.

Instead, a savvy salesperson will work to get you comfortable, perhaps asking about your day or even picking up on your body's cues about how you are feeling. If you are feeling harassed, he might sympathize with you. If you are in a festive mood, he might enhance that feeling by being equally expressive, hence building a feeling of camaraderie between the two of you.

Then, he will move onto asking questions and making the meeting about you and fulfilling your needs. Many salespeople's mistakes are talking about themselves rather than allowing their clients to talk about their needs and wants. Always make it about the person you are trying to persuade. Asking questions and listening to the target makes them think that you care about their needs and wants; you respect their beliefs and, thus, have their best interest at heart. It creates conditions where this person is more likely to actively listen to what you have to say and be persuaded.

Even when the conditions are prime for stating your point, remain subtle. There is a notion in marketing that people are less likely to buy when they know they are being sold. The same applies to the art of persuasion. Suppose a person knows that you are actively trying to change their point of view. In that case, if that is plainly stated, the person will likely put up mental guards to prevent them from being persuaded even if the material being imparted is helpful to them. A person is more likely to be persuaded if their guards are down. Therefore, you need to be low key about how you impart your persuasion. That is not mean that there are not instances where being blatant with persuasion does not work, but most often, the subtle route yields faster and better results. Subtle methods of persuasion include storytelling, drawing comparisons, and recognizing the integrity of the target.

It is also essential that you learn and understand to agree with your target even when you disagree with their view. You will never see you agree with anyone every time, and that applies to the target of your persuasion as well. While you must agree with your target as often as possible to indicate that you value their opinion, it is also okay to disagree at times. It would be best if you disagreed since you are trying to convince the target to take on a different perspective. The key is to do so diplomatically and respectfully. Keep your posture and body language open and engaging. An agreeable attitude must be maintained even when you are disagreeing.

Chapter 21. Methods of Persuasion and Tricks Used By Mass Media And Advertising

Usage of Force

The manipulator may decide to use some degree of force to successfully persuade the victim to think in some specific way. It is, however, dependent on the situation at that particular moment. It is seen to be deployed in instances where both the manipulator's ideas and the victim do not seem to match up. The type of conversation they are having don't seem to bear fruit, or where the subject appears to be irritated or frustrated with the turn the conversation has taken. It may be classified as a scare tactic by most since it gives the victim minimal time to think logically of the events that seem to be transpiring instead of when the victim is in a normal state of mind.

A manipulator is usually inclined to use force as a method of persuasion, generally at that particular instance, when they may have hit a wall on their journey of persuasion. They may also do this if the manipulator feels as though he is losing control of the grasp he had on the victim or when the victim presents them with solid evidence of the manipulator contradicting them.

Asking Leading Questions

Another method that a dark manipulator skillfully uses is to ask leading questions. It could be considered one of the strongest verbal techniques because they ask the victims questions to obtain a specific set of responses. For example, a dark persuader may ask their target, "How bad do you think these people are?" This issue already means that the individuals at issue are certainly bad to a certain extent. Dark persuaders ask these leading questions such skillfully that they instantly feel the victim is whipped up to leave the vessel and only go back to the questioning line where the victim appears to be in a relaxed position. Dark manipulators also use their real intentions to mask dark persuasion. To be easily exposed to dark persuasion, the dark manipulator hides his true intentions from the outset. Otherwise, he will fail. Skilled persuaders may mask their real intentions in several ways, depending on the individual victim and circumstance.

Create a Need

If it is executed professionally, the victim will be eating out of the persuader's palm in no time. It means that the manipulator will need to tap into their victims' fundamental needs, such as their need for self-actualization. In most cases, this technique will work well for the manipulator because the victim will need these things. For example, food is usually something that we as humans need to survive, and a prolonged lack will cause a big problem

Utilizing Illustrative and Words

The choice of words one chooses to use comes a long way in the success of using persuasion. There are many ways in which you can phrase sentences when talking about one thing. Saying the right words in the right way will make all the difference when attempting to use persuasion.

Tricks Used by Mass Media and Advertising

The media uses two main methods to persuade the masses. The first is through the use of images, and secondly, the use of sounds.

Media Persuasion by the Use of Images

Our sighs and visual processing areas of the brain are very powerful. Just think about it for a minute. Have you ever thought of a person without ending up picturing how they look? It is because of this that makes imagery and visual manipulation a preferred method by the media. Companies will often include split-second images of their product or individuals inserted into an advertisement that seems quite innocent by face value. It is usually a form of subliminal persuasion.

Media Persuasion by the Use of Sound

Sound is yet another trick that is used by the media in the persuasion of unsuspected victims. Some people usually underestimate the powers that exist within the sound. But how will you answer this? How many times have you listen or heard a song somewhere only to have it loop through your mind continuously? Songs usually influence us even though we are not aware of it despite knowing we are listening. It is what the media tends to exploit in their quest for persuasion of the masses. An example of this is seen at McDonald's. The melody "I love it" is often repeated in a manner that persuades the victims to purchase their meals continually.

Chapter 22. The Benefits of Learning About Persuasion

Your power of position will be one of the easiest ways to have persuasion. People with more real or perceived power will have more influence. However, people with power tend to talk more than others, interrupt conversations, and force the conversation to go in specific directions, thus damaging the power of their position. A person who controls their power of persuasion by engaging in meaningful dialogue can be even more influential.

Emotional control is critical. Letting your emotions run your conversation can be detrimental to your influence, but allowing emotion to pepper your argument or persuasion can be powerful. Think about how best to show your passion for your perspective or way of thinking and use it wisely. Sometimes, a well-placed expletive or watery eye can showcase how deeply you feel about what you are speaking about. Sobbing or turning red while cursing is the opposite. No matter how knowing you are on a topic, being too emotional can degrade your authority quickly.

Passion links well with expertise. When a person is knowledgeable and well prepared and passionate, they are an almost unstoppable persuasion force. It is especially helpful if you are not in a position of power in the conversation. It is a terrible truth that experts can be ignored if they cannot communicate their knowledge well, and people with little experience can be followed because they can sway a crowd with a stirring oration.

The final pillar of persuasion in communication includes controlling the connection. It is not the most powerful pillar, but it is essential. It is not just through conversation and verbal information but over your body language and understanding how others present themselves.

When you are dedicated to communicating with people, you need to be aware of these pillars of persuasion and control almost any situation with the correct words or actions. The following are here to guide you in understanding how different conversational tactics can provide you with the ultimate influence in any scenario.

Persuasion is a strong and valuable skill that not everyone has, but everyone should have. It comes in handy throughout your life in virtually any aspect of your existence, from sweet-talking your way into free movie tickets to convincing your boss you deserve a raise. By learning about persuasion will provide you with the following benefits:

In Your Personal Life

Your Relationship with Your Spouse

They say a good marriage or romantic relationship is all about compromise, but if you've ever been in a relationship, you know that's not always possible. You have to pick one side or the other, and why wouldn't it be your side? Far from being unfair or manipulative, having the ability to convince your significant other can improve your relationship because you have fewer fights about your disagreements and lack of compromise.

Your Relationship with Your Friends

We all have that one friend who always makes terrible life choices, and no one can get through to them and steer them towards the right path except you, that is. If you have influence and persuasion skills, don't keep them for yourself. Use them for good, not evil. Repeat these lines:

- "No, maybe you shouldn't marry that guy you just met."
- "Yes, limiting your day drinking is a wonderful idea!"
- "Please get that weird rash checked at the doctor."
- "Stop stealing from your workplace; you're going to get in trouble."

In Your Professional Life

Get Paid What You Deserve

Negotiating falls under persuasion, so really, absolutely everyone should have this skill. No matter if you're haggling at the market or talking a higher salary, you need to have the ability to convince your 'opponent' that you deserve this, and you should have it.

It's mostly applicable in the workplace, where—let's be real—no boss will ever willingly part with their money and hand it over to you. It's your job to convince them to do it. You've earned it, you deserve it, and it's rightfully yours. You have to ask for it, but you have to know-how, and persuasive skills help with that.

Earn the Trust and Respect of Your Boss

But of course, your only interaction with your boss isn't the yearly salary tug-of-war. If you're ever going to attain your career dreams and climb the corporate ladder, you need to have an excellent relationship with your boss, which means winning their respect and their trust.

You can accomplish that by becoming their go-to person. Offer your bright ideas, come up with solutions to problems the company is facing, persuade them to implement your suggestions, and that they're the contribution the company needs right now. In time, you will reap the rewards when your boss comes to consult with your first.

Be a Good Leader to Your Colleagues

To be effective in any leadership position—whether you're a manager, a team leader, etc. you need the power to convince people to:

- Do what you tell them

- Take you seriously

Your persuasive abilities will prove invaluable to a position like this if you want people to respect you, your work, and your ideas. It should be obvious for everyone that your way is the right way, and there will be minimal dissent if you have the necessary influence over them.

In Everyday Life

Persuasion is of unbelievable and utmost importance in our world today. Almost every human interaction involves an attempt to persuade or influence others to the speaker's way of thinking.

It is true, regardless of professions, age, sex, philosophical beliefs, or religion. If you can persuade other people, then you have a power that you can use to make your life better. Think about every person in your entire life who had influenced you to do your best and become successful.

Persuasive people can improve lives, avoid wars, and keep adolescents free from drugs or alcohol. However, some persuasive people can also destroy lives, start wars, and convince kids to try drugs or alcohol. That means persuasion is a powerful ability you can use for positive or negative things, depending on your motives. On the contrary, it would be best to use this power to attain self-improvement and overall growth for the entire community.

Get Out of Paying Tickets

Legally, a ticket is a mandatory consequence of breaking the law in some way, by speeding, failing to wear your seatbelt, talking on your cell while driving, etc. Practically, however, a ticket can be a negotiation, as long as you have the necessary skills.

Get into Coveted Clubs or Restaurants

How many times have you stood in line for hours to get into a popular club or restaurant, only to be turned away at the door by an unfriendly bouncer or snotty hostess? Well, let's see if you need to have a reservation. If you're persuasive enough, you can influence any menial gatekeeper and convince them to just let you through without needing to jump through fiery hoops or grease the well-meaning palms of anyone. Talk about some sweet perks!

Get Important Information

Do you feel like you're always being left out of the loop when it comes to important info among your family or group of friends? You don't have to guess what the drama is if you can convince someone to tell you, even if they promised they wouldn't.

If you can talk the talk well enough, you can convince anyone to tell you anything. Gossip from your friend preferred client sales dates from sales attendants, where they keep the extra free peanuts from the flight attendant, you get the idea. Sweet talk yourself into perks and valuable info.

Chapter 23. Dark Persuasion

The diversion between normal persuasion and dark persuasion is that dark persuasion does not always justify moral justification. While a normal persuader may try to persuade someone for that person's good, a dark persuader does so with motivations that aren't always good for the other person. They try to get a full grasp of the understanding of the person they wish to persuade, and they take pains to do so because they know what the biggest motivation is.

While persuasion always has moral implications, a dark persuader does not concern themselves with these implications. They are aware of them but choose to place their eyes on their objective(s) instead.

Persuasion is a psychological phenomenon in the everyday life of a human being. It is either that you are the one trying to persuade someone else or you are being persuaded. What makes the difference between dark and normal is the motivation behind it. In mass media, politics, advertising, and legal decisions, persuasion comes into play all the time. The outcome of practicing it in these fields is determined by ways of persuasion, which will influence the subject of persuasion.

There are some obvious and crucial differences between persuasion and other types of mind control, such as brainwashing and hypnosis. While these two requirements that the subject should be isolated to change their minds and identity, persuasion does not also require isolation.

To get to the goal, manipulation is used on one person. Although persuasion can also be done on a single subject to change their minds, there's a possibility of using it on a large scale to change a whole group's minds or even an entire society.

For this reason, persuasion is a more effective mind control technique and perhaps more dangerous because it can change the minds of many people at the same time instead of the mind of just one person at a time.

Several people make the mistake of thinking they have immunity to the effects of persuasion because they believe that they will always see every sales pitch that comes their way. They believe they will always be able to use logic to grasp what is going on and then find a logical conclusion.

Thanks to the fact that people are not always going to fall for everything they hear, this may be true if they use logic. It is also possible to avoid persuasion because the argument does not augur well with the person's beliefs, no matter the argument's strength.

Nevertheless, some people know how to use persuasive messages to encourage people to patronize the latest gadgets or products in the market. This act of persuasion is very subtle, so the subject will not always identify it, so it will be quite challenging for them to always form an opinion about the information they will get.

Every time persuasion is mentioned, one likely thinks of it in a bad light. They automatically think of a conman or salesman trying to change their perspective and eventually push them until this change is achieved.

While dark persuasion is prominent in sales and conning practices, there are also ways that persuasion can be used for good, like in diplomatic relations between international bodies or in public service campaigns. The contrast only lies in the way the process of persuasion is brought to play.

Dark Persuasion Techniques

When a person is willing to change their subject's mind by persuading them to do something contrary to their initial state of mind, the persuader will have some well laid out techniques to help them achieve their goals.

Each day that passes, the target is going to face different types of persuasion. For food makers, their goal will be to get their target to try out their new recipes or have them stick to the old ones, while studios will flash their latest blockbuster movies on the faces of their targets.

Whatever the case may be or whatever product they are selling, their main aim is to make more sales, and that is why they are trying to persuade you. They really couldn't care less about how this will impact you, and this is the reason why they must be very careful and skilled in the art of subtle persuasion to ensure that they do not tip you off or get you agitated. Since there are also many other brands trying to persuade you, they must find a unique way to impress their views on you.

Due to the influence of persuasion on a wide range of people, the techniques used in it have been studied for many years, dating back to ancient times. It is because influence is a very useful tool in the hands of a wide range of people.

Starting from the early 20th century, the formal study of these techniques began to grow. Remember that the goal of trying to persuade people is to push a persuasive argument on an audience and have them convinced. They will then internalize this message and adopt it as their new attitude or even way of life. For this point, there is a great need to discover the most successful persuasion techniques. Three dark persuasion techniques have proven to be of great value over the years.

Create a Need

It is one of the most fruitful ways of changing their perspective or way of life. The person trying to persuade a target will either create a need or capitalize on a need that the subject already has. If this is done properly, it has the potential of appealing a great deal to the target.

It means that to be successful, the persuader must appeal to the needs that are of more importance to the target. It may be their need to fulfill their dreams or boosting their self-esteem. It may also be their want for love, shelter, or food.

This method will always work out well because there is no way the subject will not need it. Since there is no way the target isn't going to have dreams and aspirations, the persuader will only have to find ways to make the victim understand how they can easily help them achieve those dreams.

The persuader may also tell their target that the target will realize their dreams if they make specific alterations to their beliefs or perspective. Doing this, according to the persuader, will give the target a higher chance of achieving success.

Appealing to Social Needs

The other technique that the persuader can use is identifying the target's social needs. While this may not yield as many results and the target's primary needs will, it is still an essential tool in the persuader's hands.

Some people are naturally drawn to crowds and desire to be wanted. They always want to have specific items, not because they need them, but because it comes with certain prestige that makes them feel like they belong to a higher class.

The notion of appealing to the target's social needs is obtainable through many TV commercials where viewers are encouraged to buy a product not to be "left behind." When they can identify and appeal to the target's social needs, the result is they can reach a new area of the target's interest.

Making Use of Loaded Words and Images

When someone is persuading someone else, they must be careful with their choice of words as words can make all the difference. While there are many ways to say a thing, one way of saying it may be more potent than the other.

When it has to do with persuasion, one of the essential things knows how to say the right thing at the right time. Words are always essential tools in communication and knowing the right call-to-action words.

Dark persuasion is one of the most powerful dark psychology concepts, but sadly it is always overlooked and underestimated. It may be because, unlike the other methods of mind control, persuasion leaves the target with a choice. In the other mind control methods, the target is forced into submission. Sometimes, this is done by putting them in isolation not to have any say in the outcome.

When it comes to persuasion, the chips are laid bare (although with an ulterior motive in dark persuasion) so that the target is left to make the decision that they think will suit them best.

Chapter 24. Covert Persuasion

Covert persuasion typically addresses the exact prediction of human behavior in any given context. Numerous attempts have been made in history to categorize people to understand them better and anticipate their behavior. A brief overview of this initiative shows various of the most famous names in psychology, consumer behavior, philosophy (NLP), and business from the periods of Aristotle, Freud, B.F. Skinner, Jung, Carl Rogers, Abraham Maslow, and William James, to the more modern brains of psychology, industry, and marketing, came up with some brilliant ways of understanding our collective thought and decision making to persuade us and influence and direct our behavior.

The Hermann Brain Superiority Predictor, the Myers Briggs Type Indicator, and the Language and Behavioral Profile are some examples of attempts to categorize us all. Of course, there are the endless personality tests that try to determine if you are well suited to a sales career. Moreover, there is the Enneagram of individuality and, obviously, the traditional 4-quadrant explanation of us as a Relator, Socializer, Thinker, or Director.

There is a famous theory that all of our actions stem from our need to avoid grief and attain pleasure. But it's not as easy as that. There's also the whole area of language analysis where it's assumed the words you're using will dictate your feelings. The labels (words) you put on your experiences determine your emotions.

Examples of Great People Manifesting Effectiveness of Covert Persuasion

Everything you have or will ever get, become, do, or learn, you'll get with and through others. Life is but persuasion! The world is the perfect context for persuasion and convincing. Marketers and advertisers are making virtually endless attempts to understand every one of us accurately. Every year they will spend hundreds of millions of dollars trying to catch our attention, convince us to buy their product or service, sample their offer, vote for their candidate, and donate to their cause. In reality, if you live in the US, each year, you alone are the recipient of more than $3,200 of marketing and advertising messages. That's a lot of money that's invested in convincing people.

Persuasion techniques help you understand and apply these to achieve your goals in the real world. Starting with the self-talk inside your mind that is important for the trust required to manipulate others, all the way to the final action of communicating straight to the one you want to convince, your target, are all here.

Through mastering the powers of persuasion, you will find it easy to get more of what you want and when you want. If you are in sales, you will now have tools at your disposal, which will double or even triple your profits and commissions if you consciously and regularly put the ideas and techniques to use every day in your work life. It sounds insane, but you're not going to be in the first 1,000 to tell us this was what happened. If you're in business, you have to convince colleagues, managers, and superiors to go along with your proposals. Here you will find plenty of methods that you can use instantly to persuade others to think your way covertly.

Persuasion strategies also include phrases that are more convincing when it comes to your personal and business life. Combining these terms with powerful stories will help you convince more people, more often.

The strategies and techniques would encourage you to have more of what you want more often by subtly or covertly persuading the other person to think your way. It doesn't take any more time to achieve it; however, you get everything you want, and you don't have to compromise or give up anything.

The persuasion methods often consist of powerful hidden powers like emotions and the influence of well-structured, well-thought-out, result-based questions.

Persuasion starts in the mind. Many words are written about how the human brain works, and many different opinions and hypotheses on how we think precisely. Yet, one thing is sure. To convince someone else to believe your way, you have to sync your mind with theirs. Effective persuasion begins and ends when a "mind meld" of real meaning, emotion, and comprehension is present. So how do we create this mind meld? How do we become more adept at persuading other people to think our way? The answer lies in knowing what motivates the other person and pushes him. Equipped with that experience, you can organize your thoughts and demands so that other individuals with little or no questions can easily and quickly embrace them. They will see you as much as they do and feel compelled to satisfy your requests.

Persuasion bypasses the vital human mind component without the message recipient being aware of the process. It is a question of getting through both resistance and response. It is achieved when one person sends a message, and it is received from the recipient without any critical thinking or questioning.

Persuasion is sometimes about controlling and handling the "state." What is the state of mind of that other person? For example, in the selling atmosphere, the consumer does not have to buy the product or service; in fact, purchasing is not an indication that there has been Covert Persuasion. An individual without money could easily be convinced and put in a purchase state, whereas he did not have the money.

Chapter 25. Ethical Persuasion

With persuasion and manipulation so closely related and only differentiated in a few key ways, you may be wondering how to keep your persuasion ethical. You may even be wondering why anyone would want to persuade, even ethically. There is a simple reason for this: Persuading others can often be quite beneficial to the other person, especially when you do so to better the other. Think of the best leader you may have ever encountered in your life. Perhaps it was a teacher that just had a way about him that always swayed people to behave. His very presence was enough to keep even the most troublesome students in line, even though those students rarely wanted actually to be in class. He could genuinely keep people involved in class and appeal to everyone, keeping even the students who would largely avoid learning in school engaged. He was able to do this through the persuasion of his own. Does this make the teacher a bad person? Not at all—he knew how best to deliver his messages to his targets, and in doing so, he was able to persuade those around him to pay attention.

Ethical persuasion can be used in a wide range of situations; it can be used with your children to keep them behaving well. It can be used at work to defuse stressful situations. It can be used to come to some agreement with a spouse or friend. There are endless possibilities for ethical persuasion if you are willing to give it a chance.

Remaining Ethical

While it may seem challenging to juggle ethics when attempting to persuade someone else of something, there is a helpful anagram to help you: TARES. It stands for truthfulness, authenticity, respect, equity, and social responsibility. When you keep this in mind while attempting to persuade those around you, you will be better able to keep your behavior in check. Remember, persuasion, in the right context, can be beneficial to everyone involved. It does not have to be avoided simply because it falls within the same category of social influences as manipulation. If done correctly, persuasion is a powerful tool that will enable you to continue to act ethically while still persuading someone else to do what you see is right.

Truthfulness

When you test your persuasion and intent, start first with analyzing the truthfulness of what you are saying. You want to remain truthful and honest when attempting to persuade those around you for a good reason—you want the other person to be informed. When staying ethical, you should recognize the other person as their person with their own free will that deserves respect, just as you would want for yourself. You would not want someone else infringing upon your own free will, and as such, you should make it a point not to infringe on the free will of others either.

When testing for truthfulness, ask yourself if what you have said is true. Beyond that, though, you must ask yourself if you have omitted any information you felt would negatively influence the person or keep the person away from acting in the way you would prefer him or her to do so. You must make sure that you are truthful in your communication as well as in your lack of communication—make sure you leave no pertinent information out, regardless of whether the other person has asked about it or not. You want to make sure that the other person is as informed as possible because you want the other person to willingly agree to do what you ask without coercion and manipulation.

Authenticity

The other test for ethical persuasion is determining the authenticity of what is being presented. At a glance, this may seem similar to verifying truthfulness, but it goes a little further. In truthfulness, the important part was making sure that everything was accurate and reported wholly and truthfully. With authenticity, you are checking the integrity of the message you are trying to convey. You must ask yourself whether you are doing what you are doing with good intentions. It means that you are not stereotyping, generalizing, or using fear to scare the person into an agreement with you.

Ultimately, you must make sure that the message you are conveying is done for good reasons. An easy and straightforward way to test for this is to ask if you would buy into it if you were presented with just the information on its own. For example, if you are trying to persuade someone to buy a car and you were in that person's situation, such as buying a family car that will fit three car seats, would you take the message you are presenting as honest, authentic, and trustworthy? If you feel as though you would agree with the reasoning being provided, the message is likely authentic. If you think that you may have a problem with the information presented, you should probably reevaluate the situation and your behavior and words. To make sure you are lining your persuasion up with ethics.

Respect

Then, you want to evaluate to make sure you are acting and persuading with respect. Are you recognizing the individual needs of the person you are attempting to persuade? Is what you are saying something that you would be comfortable announcing to other people as well, or would you be embarrassed or ashamed to be trying to persuade a perfect stranger of the message you are delivering? For example, if you aim to persuade someone to buy a minivan, are you appealing to some gender stereotype, or are you genuinely offering up the benefits a van has to offer entirely neutrally, such as talking about how spacious the seats are and how nice it is to have doors that slide open instead of swinging open when trying to keep track of kids.

Suppose you feel that your message hinges upon something stereotypical in any way or are not tailored to the individual. In that case, you are attempting to target with your persuasion, and you should probably look into ways to change the message. Just ensure that what you are attempting to persuade the other person is not offensive, nor is it done offensively. For example, you should not say that the other person must not be educated because they are from a specific minority with a lower rate of higher education. Because of that, they likely want this one specific car that many lower-educated minorities ask for. That would not be appropriate in this situation—it does not respect the individual as a person and is not respectful in general. Avoid the stereotypes and seek to get to know and understand the individual you are helping to ensure that the information you present is as relevant, respectful, and persuasive as possible.

Equity

The fourth step in analyzing your persuasion, then, is equity. When you are attempting to ensure that your message is equitable, you seek to ensure that both you and the other person are on an even playing field. It is incredibly essential that you are not looking to lead by coercion or by playing upon the other person's ignorance. You should seek to make sure that you are offering up as much information as possible to ensure that they feel that an informed decision is possible when trying to persuade the other person.

Often, when people attempt to persuade others, they play off of a lack of information. When someone is misinformed, it is much easier to take advantage of that misinformation. For example, if someone came in for medical treatment and asked for something far more expensive and far more than the person needed, it would be unethical for the doctor to accept that without ever talking about less invasive options appropriate for treatment. You want to do the same and precisely with your persuasion. Back to the example of the car salesperson, if you have someone coming in to trade in his car because he has hit 100,000 miles and the person has always heard that after 100,000 miles, the car is no longer reliable and needs to be replaced. As a salesperson, you may have thought it would be the perfect opportunity to get in an extra sale. Still, as the conversation continues, you learn that the person is not in a good place to get a new car but felt that he had to do so merely because of the mileage, even though everything was working correctly. It would be unethical not to point out the information you know would keep the person from buying the car because not pointing that out would only take advantage of his lack of information on the topic. That is not equitable—the other person deserves an even playing field when making decisions, even if giving that information can cause the person to decide against what you are attempting to persuade him to do in the first place.

Social Responsibility

Finally, the last method to check for ethical persuasion is social responsibility. It is when you stop to see if your persuasion is beneficial advice as a whole. If it is not, how can you change how you are persuading to ensure that you are doing so in a way that protects those who may be at a disadvantage? Remember, the point of persuasion is to convince people to do things on their own—it is not intended to be harmful to other people, nor should it cause others distress.

Suppose your persuasion is generally a good thing and will not have negative implications to the world at large, for example. In that case, you are not persuading someone to think of something in a racially biased manner, and it has passed through all of the other steps, then your persuasion method is likely to sound, and you are free to move forward with it. If it failed anywhere along the way, you would likely want to make sure that you are working to make your persuasion methods more ethical. Remember, ethics are respectful. They treat people with basic human decency, something that everyone deserves.

Chapter 26. Difference Between Persuasion and Negotiation

What Is Negotiation?

Negotiation is a way of resolving differences. It is a mechanism through which consensus or agreement is achieved while disagreements and conflicts are avoided. In any conflict, people understandably try to accomplish the best result (or perhaps an entity they represent) for their status. However, the foundations for a successful outcome are the core values of fairness, mutual benefit, and relationship maintenance.

In many situations, specific negotiation types are being used in international affairs, law, administration, industrial disputes, or intra-regional relations. But in a variety of activities, overall negotiation skills could be managed to learn and applied. Negotiation experience can help solve the conflicts between you and anyone.

Negotiation Phases

A formal negotiation strategy can be beneficial in securing a favorable outcome. For instance, in a job situation, it may be appropriate to schedule a conference where all the parties concerned will interact. The negotiation process contains the following phases:

Preparedness

A decision must be made before discussions. About when and where to talk about the issue and who will be involved. It is also beneficial to establish a limited period to avoid more conflicts. This phase consists of making sure all the relevant facts are known to explain your position. In the above example, the knowledge of your organization's "rules" for which assistance is given is included when aid is not deemed appropriate and the reasons for such refusals. The rules you can adhere to in preparing talks may be in the organization. While addressing the dispute, planning can help prevent future disagreements and unintentionally waste time during the session.

Talk of the Matter

Individuals or representatives of each side put the case as they choose, i.e., their awareness of the situation, forward during this stage. In this step, key skills involve interviewing, listening, and explanation. It is sometimes helpful to note all points rose during the debate stage if further clarification is necessary. Listening is essential, as it is simple to make the error that you talk too much and listen too little when there is conflict. Each hand should have the same chance of presenting its case.

Objectives Clarity

The aims, interests, and views of the dispute's two fronts must be clarified from the discussion. Such considerations should be identified as objectives. Through this explanation, absolute mutual respect can often be found or created. Clarification is an integral part of the negotiation phase. Unless it is overlooked, difficulties and challenges to obtaining a positive outcome can occur.

Discuss the Win-Win Results

In this phase, a win-win situation is focused on where the two parties feel their views are considered. This phase concentrates on what is called a win-win output. Generally, the best result is a win-win outcome. It may not always be feasible, but this should be the final goal through mediation. Various strategies and sacrifices suggestions need to be considered here. Commitments are often positive choices, often more beneficial than holding the initial positions for all concerned.

Agreement

Accord can be established after attention has been extended to recognizing the opinions and desires of both parties. To reach an acceptable outcome, everyone concerned must remain open-minded. Any contract must be made clear so that the decisions have been taken on both sides. The intervention plan must be followed to carry out the determination under the agreement.

Non-Agreement

If the negotiation process breaks down, and no agreement is reached, another meeting is expected. It prohibits both sides from engulfing themselves in warm debates or disputes that not only bother wasting time but can also affect future interactions. The negotiation phases should always be repeated at the upcoming meeting. Some new ideas or desires must be addressed, and the condition revisited. It could also be useful to look at alternatives and to mediate in another individual.

Informal Discussions

Sometimes, more unofficially, it is necessary to negotiate. In those cases, it might be difficult or essential to take the above steps officially if there is a disagreement. However, in various casual settings, it can be beneficial to remember the main points in the stage of formal negotiations.

The following three components are essential and will likely affect the outcome of negotiations in any talks:

Attitudes

The attitudes to the system itself, for instance, attitudes towards problems and individuals involved with the individual case or attitudes aligned with social acknowledgment requirements, have strongly influenced all conversation. Know always that: mediation is not a place for personal successes to be accomplished. The need to bargain with the government can be resentful. Through bargaining, characteristics may affect the actions of a human, such as that of individuals.

Awareness

The more awareness you have of the issues concerned, the greater your involvement in the negotiation process. Well-preparedness is essential, in other words.

Gain as much knowledge about your assignments as possible about the issues. Therefore, it is essential to understand how things are resolved because mediation can require different approaches in various situations.

Interpersonal Competencies

Strong interpersonal skills are important to successful talks, informal settings, and non-formal or less formal or one-to-one meetings. Such competencies include:

- Successful verbal contact

- Hearing

- Project study

- Solving question

- I am deciding

- Stability

- Tackling difficult circumstances

Are Negotiation and Persuasion the Same?

Negotiation is defined as two, or even more, people interact to reach an agreement on one or more issues and talk with another person to agree.

Persuasion can be described as the act or method of manipulating or moving to a new opinion, place, or course of action–through argument or intercession. It's the key to all discussions to transfer somebody to a new post or action path. Throughout immobilization negotiations, two parties try to find a compromise. It is mainly the case. While anyone may try to negotiate, an efficient and persuasive negotiator typically works more successfully.

Bringing up persuasion as a negotiation strategy means looking at the various types of conviction values related to property transactions; there are six different opportunities for self-interest, individuality, comparison, swap, sameness, and logical sense in property negotiations.

In the other perfect world, everybody would agree with you, and you would still be correct. About 99% of the time is not like that. What are you doing? Frequently people use manipulation to manipulate their stance on the other side. Persuasion is perfect if it succeeds because it does not cost you much but often does not succeed, so that you may have to bargain. So, what the distinction between persuasion and bargaining is.

It is best to switch to a dictionary to describe persuasion. The meaning 'to persuade' of Merriam-Webster is 'to compel (somebody) to do something by questioning, debating, and giving reasons.'

A brilliant short book called "Eristic Dialectic, the Art of Being Wrong" has been published by Arthur Schopenhauer and is still one of the day's popular rhetoric. Its 38 stratagems educate you about using logical errors, false proposals, generalization, and other handy instruments. There are some essential differences in both processes: the point of persuasion is to say, and trade is a negotiation. Strategies of persuasion are to explain, to promote, to manipulate, to inspire, to argue, to advise, and to contest.

On the other hand, negotiation implies that concerns, desires, shortcomings, motivations, and goals can be considered so that a better understanding can be made available from both sides. There is not strictly exclusive convincing and mediation either.

Both could be close to their results or goal. All strategies are very successful, and citizens are often persuaded that they prefer their reasoning and beliefs above compromise. The other party's reasoning and views tend to us not to be particularly interested. The individual may find it difficult to change his position, but we still choose it as persuading is which we've developed with since childhood and used again. Negotiation is challenging because we must be attentive to the other party's views, values, and reasoning and consider ways of dealing with them.

If we speak about compromise, there is some uncertainty about whether we say mediation or coercion. Negotiations, in their very essence, warrant a rapprochement between the two sides to reach a compromise. Convincing or manipulating, though, is the process of making the other party do what they want.

The Art of Convincing Is Often Termed Negotiation

Good negotiation leverage you will learn when and how to use effective skills to be a good negotiator. It is probably happening at times when you seem unable to agree on negotiations. In these cases, it is also necessary to understand how and when to persuade efficiently.

Use of Queries to Help Persuade Others to Compromise

Comments are high as they speak to the other arm. Yet reacting to what is being said is the real art of interrogation. It doesn't mean that you hang on each word. "The detection, selection, and interpretation of keywords that turn information into intelligence" is the definition of Mullender's listening. His conceptual model is 'information you use for your benefit.'

In sales situations, implied and explicit requirements are the keywords that a client of our SPIN Selling Skills model would listen to. An effective sales representative can turn that information in the form of profit statements into intelligence.

The profit statement requires that sellers dive into issues or perceived concerns, precisely the same as that recommended by Mullender, to "steer anxiety" in circumstances of recovery. You will define the specific desires (what the other side wants to do about this) and render helpful suggestions only by finding the real source of the pain. Unsurprisingly, in these cases, Mullender points to SPIN as a "stunningly clever" template.

Ultimately, while talks can be seen as a separate part of a process and a different ability to sell/persuade, a successful leader must still be willing in a negotiating scenario to execute suitable persuasive techniques. They recommend that negotiators develop strong selling strategies and negotiation skills to help them produce win-win outcomes. It is why they support

What Should You Select?

Seek first to convince and see whether it fits for you. Though, we were all on the other hand of someone who told us constantly that we don't approve. It cannot be very pleasant. Although persuading and bargaining, know when you hit an impasse.

The persuasion of sound is always stronger than the power of language. When you have the point of no-return, substitute the tone to be more convincing or switch your bargaining dialogue—you are much more likely to get a response. The persuasion of sound is always better than the persuasion of words.

Chapter 27. Deception

When someone is trying to deceive another person, the intentions are usually going to be pretty bad. It is a useful tool for being a dark manipulator, but you have to remember that most people will not be happy if they find out it is being used against them.

Perceiving Deception

Suppose the subject is enthused about maintaining a strategic distance from deception in their life to keep up a key decent way from the mind games that go with it. In that case, it is as frequently as conceivable a sharp plan to understand how to recognize when deception is going on. Reliably, it is difficult for the subject to find that deception is going on, except for if the master goofs and lies are clear or noticeable, or they repudiate something that the subject undeniably knows to be genuine. While it might be difficult for the chairman to cheat the subject for an important stretch, it will, by and large, happen in typical ordinary nearness between people who know one another. Recognizing when deception happens is regularly hazardous, considering the path that there few pointers that are completely solid to tell when deception occurs.

Techniques Used in Deception

Deception is a type of expression that utilizes lies and omissions to persuade the victim to fit into the world that the agent wants. A form of interaction or communication has to be involved. Deception can manifest itself in different types, according to the situation where it is applied. It is challenging to tell when someone is trying to deceive others. Luckily, though, there are a few components that, when identified, point to the likelihood of deception being involved. After many years of studying deception, psychologists have developed three classifications of deception: camouflage, simulation, and disguise. Out of the three classifications of deception, we can identify the common techniques used in deception. Let us first define the classifications.

Camouflage

Camouflage is the first classification of deception. The deceiver works to conceal the truth of their intentions in a way that the subject cannot decode. Just like the typical camouflage deployed by animals and plants to hide from predators or to approach prey without being detected, deceivers make use of methods that are hard to detect without extra observation.

Simulation

The second classification of deception is simulation. Simulation is the act of imitating to be something. In deception, simulation is defined as exposing the victim to false information as a tool of misleading them. There are three types of simulation described below.

Fabrication

Fabrication means altering reality. The deceiver can use a real thing and change it to work in their favor. For example, they can add or reduce details to a story to make it better or worse to convince the subject. A real-life example is when a suspect in court over stealing tells the judge that they stole food because they were almost starving, yet they intended to sell their loot for financial gain.

Mimicry

The second type of simulation is known as mimicry. Mimicry is defined as the art of imitating to ridicule or confuse a situation. In deception, mimicry happens when the deceiver pretends to be something or someone that they are not. A deceiver might steal an idea from someone, and instead of citing the owner; they use it as their own. An example of mimicry is when an author uses a famous writer's name to fool readers to purchase their book.

Distraction

The final type of simulation is called distraction. Distraction is the act of cunningly forcing the victim to shift their attention from reality and focus on falsehood. To divert the subject, a deceiver can use a form of bait, which might appear to be more convincing or beneficial than the truth.

Disguise

The third classification of deception is a disguise. Disguise is defined as the act of faking a different appearance to conceal one's identity. When it is being deployed, the deceiver puts up the impression of being somebody or something different from what they are. Practically, disguise means the agent keeps something from the victim, as their intentions, what they do for a living, etc.

Lies

A lie refers to the agent's act in making up and feeding the victim information that is not true. When presenting a lie, the deceiver makes it appear as a fact, thereby making the subject absorb it as the truth. Lies are the most common techniques used in deception since they divert the victim from verifiable facts and make them easy targets of manipulation.

Concealment

Concealment is the act of preventing something from being recognized. In deception, it is mostly deployed by the use of half-truths. While giving information, the deceiver intentionally omits some essential parts to keep some truth from the receiver. While the deceiver will not have lied to the victim directly, they will have ensured that the most important information has been kept from them.

Creating Illusions

Deceivers are experts at creating convincing illusions. Once they have acquired the subject's attention, they demonstrate imaginary pictures that sway them into partnering with them. They come up with illusions that appear to be realistic and workable in every way. The first step of creating the illusions is to explain their "ideas" to the target's mind. After that, they pull back a little to wait and see if the subject will develop an interest in the illusions.

Equivocations

Waffling is the application of ambiguous language to hide the truth. Ambiguous language can be indirect or contradictory. The equivocations' objective is to confuse the victim, so they are not aware of what is happening. If a deceiver is asked a question, he avoids giving definite answers and provides general responses. They can also be used by the deceiver to escape blame if they are found out. If they are suspected, they give many explanations about whose aim is to confuse the accuser.

Understatements

An understatement is a situation that has been minimized but can cause more effects than what has been portrayed. The deceiver delivers a statement to their victim while making it appear like a small deal than what it is. However, the statement can influence the victim more than they have been made to believe.

Exaggeration

Exaggeration is the opposite of an understatement. It is whereby a situation is overstretched or overstated to alter it. The deceiver might not be lying directly to the victim, but they turn a situation into a far bigger deal than it is. Exaggerations can be used to convince the victim in a situation where they would not be, had they been given the genuine version of the situation.

Seduction

Seduction is typical on social media, where a person can write an attractive bio about themselves and top it up with carefully processed photos or videos to catch others' attention. The problem is that both the bio and the media provided by such people might be false and only intended to lure followers or lovers.

Rationalization

Rationalization is the deployment of weak or far-fetched arguments with the intent of convincing someone that something is more pleasant than it appears. In the context of deception, the agent comes up with clear ideas to convince the victim to do something difficult to accept or is unpleasant under normal circumstances.

Playing the Servant

Another method used to deceive people is playing the volunteer or servant role. In this case, the deceiver hides their agenda by making their victims believe that they are doing something for a noble cause. The subjects are less likely to suspect that someone is up to some mischief, who claims to be doing something to assist others. Therefore, they end up trusting them and concurrently lowering their defense mechanisms. Once the deceivers have their way, they unravel their evil plans.

Diversion

Diversion is the action of changing the natural or acceptable course of something. In deception, diversion is a tricky endeavor that aims at destroying a subject. Mind controllers are aware of the human traits which direct their responses, behaviors, and personalities, such as self-esteem and discipline.

Playing the Victim

Deception takes a lot of consideration for emotions. A deceiver uses playing victims to appear weaker or hurt, whereas they are the ones in control. The idea is to make others believe that they are victims of circumstances to evoke sympathy, compassion, and pity from the people they look forward to deceiving. Once a victim shows some form of concern for the deceiver, they cooperate with them and become easy to deceive.

Chapter 28. The Dark Triad

Often, abusers fall within this category—the dark triad. The dreaded three personality types combine to create a human storm capable of destroying lives so utterly that the individuals have little hope of reassembling them without intensive professional assistance. These personality types are dark—they do not care about people and encompass everything wrong, and everything toxic about humanity. They are often monstering within human skin, staring out into the world, and looking to wreak as much havoc as they can as quickly as possible. These three traits are Machiavellianism, narcissism, and psychopathy. They are dangerous enough on their own, but when you find an individual who harnesses them all, be forewarned—you are better off leaving while you still can and escaping all of the nonsense altogether as quickly as possible.

Machiavellianism

If you had to simplify Machiavellianism into the shortest possible phrase— "The ends justify the means." Though never directly stated by Niccolò Machiavelli, an Italian politician and philosopher from the 1500s, this phrase came from the text he wrote in The Prince in 1513. He informed the prince that was being instructed within the document to present himself in one way, honest and benevolent, even though he was ready to behave as harshly as necessary because everyone can see a person. But very few people will ever actually get close enough to realize the truth. The message is essentially summed up by saying that the ends justify the means, meaning that it was acceptable to lie because it made the prince more well-liked. A well-liked leader is far more likely to be a successful leader that can maintain power.

Drawing from that principle, Machiavellian people are adept at appearing how those around them wish to see them. They will say whatever those around them want to hear because they know that it is unlikely that those around them will ever know the truth, and telling them what they want to hear makes them happier and gets the Machiavellian person what he or she wants. Then, getting the desired result, the end justifies the means of lying, even though lying is typically considered morally wrong and reprehensible.

This personality type is quite insidious—you never know whether you see what you are getting. The Machiavellian individual is deceitful and a master at deceiving people around him or her. They will only tell the truth if it is beneficial to them or is the most desired result, which it usually is not. They assume that it is more important to seem desirable and make good connections than developing proper relationships. Still, when you see people as nothing more than a means to an end, you are not likely to ever want to develop a relationship with others. When people are nothing but means they have been dehumanized, it turned into nothing but tools to be utilized to get what you want in any way possible simply because you want that result. Ultimately, despite the immorality of the behavior, you will do whatever it is that you must get the result you wish to only because it will get you what you want, and that is all you care about at the end of the day.

These people should never be trusted—they always have an ulterior motive, no matter how truthful they may seem in the moment. There is always something motivating them to behave in specific ways; whether it is innocent or not is up for debate. You are better off avoiding and not trusting this person whenever possible.

Narcissism

The other one is the narcissist—those with narcissism have a narcissistic personality disorder. It is characterized when an individual present with a grandiose sense of self, meaning he is quite egotistical and believes that he is far superior to a pervasive lack of empathy and an excessive need for admiration and attention. The narcissist thrives off of getting his or her sense of self-justified through actions such as praise or admiration—they only see themselves as worthwhile if others around see them as worthwhile first. They want to be recognized as worthy and will do whatever it takes to get that.

It means that narcissists are often willing to lie about who they are or what they like. They have no true sense of self beyond someone that desperately seeks the approval and admiration of others, no matter what the cost, and is willing to do whatever it takes to get it, even if that means lying about who they are.

The narcissist typically creates an alter ego of sorts, a persona that he presents to the world that is everything he wishes he was—charismatic, powerful, influential, and well-liked. He then utilizes several dark psychology manipulation techniques to keep people under the spell he seeks to create. He creates a sense of self and then always plays mind games and manipulates those around him. Only those who get close to the narcissist to be trapped in his web of lies beyond hope of getting out ever see his true self. The malicious individual lies beneath the persona, lurking for the first possible chance to lash out at those around him.

After snaring a victim within his trap, he will systematically manipulate the other person, conditioning them into doing whatever the narcissist desires. Over time, he can mold his victim into the perfect source of constant admiration, something referred to as his narcissistic supply. He will then always utilize manipulation and mind control techniques to keep his new toy under his thumb for as long as possible, attempting to break down his victim by any means necessary systematically.

Psychopathy

Psychopaths suffer from their personality disorders, in which they are often characterized through a series of persistent antisocial actions. They almost always lack any real sense of empathy—the innate human ability to connect emotionally with others at any meaningful level. This lack of empathy makes them incredibly dangerous. Without empathy, which is a built-in red flag system that lets us understand when something is wrong with those around us, particularly in regards to our behaviors to others, the psychopath has no real fail-safe to his or her behaviors—he will continue to push and push, even with the most aggressive behaviors, simply because he does not feel any need to stop. For those who do feel empathy, the pain they, themselves, feel as they harm someone else is usually enough to make them stop. The pain and guilt become overwhelming, and they stop before making it worse. The psychopath, however, does not feel that.

Beyond the lack of empathy and, therefore, remorse, psychopaths typically exhibit disinhibited behaviors—in simpler words, they are impulsive. A thought will pop into their mind with some random impulse, such as stealing a purse from someone or deciding to hurt another person, and they are far more likely to act upon it simply because they like to act upon their impulses.

Psychopaths are frequently also bold—they do not fear anything they are approached with. Consequences are not intimidating. People are not intimidating. Even dying or being harmed is not intimidating to the psychopath. The psychopath is incredibly tolerant of danger and is frequently noticed to have high confidence and assertiveness. Even though he is not likely to want to do anything meaningful with that confidence—he sees no point in engaging in social conventions.

The Dark Triad

With those three personality types now described in an easy-to-understand manner, you may now be wondering what happens when the three are combined. The results are an aggressive, toxic individual who does not care to act in a normal manner. They are fantastic at exploitation, lacking the empathy necessary to impede such negative, harmful behavior, and having the right amount of lack of impulse control to encourage it. They manipulate, they hurt, they steal, and they lie. They are callous, meaning they do not care about others' feelings and revel in seeing people hurt, angry, or sad. Research has shown that people with the dark triad personality type all enjoyed seeing people with negative expressions on their faces.

Ultimately, those possessing the dark triad are not forces to be reckoned with—they will do anything that will hurt you if you wrong them, and they do not care enough about social conventions to be held back from seriously harming you.

Chapter 29. How To Analyze People

It is the knowledge of the character by the features of the face and hand. It is about moving from an empirical art to an observation science. The character is not independent of the physical constitution. The state of our body conditions it. On the other hand, the body is influenced by the emotions of the soul.

Life is due to a double movement: a dilation movement and a conservation movement, which analyzes any human being's personality.

The Dilation-Expansion

Its adaptability characterizes it to the environment, an externalization of intuitive and affective tendencies, sociability, cheerful humor, need to be in groups, intelligence adapted to the useful and directed to practical realizations.

The Conservation-Seclusion

Oppositely manifests itself, with an elective adaptation to a privileged environment. Since withdrawal is a defense process, it acts only in a medium that does not suit you.

While the expansive individual is a friend of the whole world, disperses his activity in all directions, reacts impulsively, is determined, and has a sensory intelligence of immediate contact, the withdrawn has only friends of choice. If he does not have them, he prefers loneliness, concentrates, and is only active in some directions. It is not resolved unless he has reflected, does not trust his sensory impressions, and is more idealistic, replacing reality with abstractions, distrusting his senses, and reason.

The Expansive Individual

It is characterized by having a thick structure, colored and warm skin, wide round face, largemouth, snub nose, large eyes, and a smiling expression, with ease and abundance of exchanges.

The Retracted Individual

It is thin in nature, short limbs, dry and cold skin, and pale dye. The face is elongated, narrow, and bony. It is economical, selective in the exchanges, smallmouth, narrow and bony nose, sunken eyes, hermetic face, and little communicative.

The Expansive-Retracted

It is an intermediate of the recent two; the face is rectangular, large eyes slightly sunken. It opens or closes, depending on the situation.

Physiological Tricks to Analyzing People

In valuing people we have just met, we are often victims of our psychological mechanisms. It can lead to misunderstandings and preconceptions that eventually affect our ability to socialize. The best way to counteract these mistakes is to know how to identify them, so here are the common mistakes we make when valuing others.

Confuse Personality and Situations

When we observe someone's specific behavior, we immediately think that they act according to their personality. Instead, when we think about our behavior, we usually value it based on the situation in which we find ourselves.

For example, we know that we are distant when we are worried about something. However, if a person you just met acts in this way, you may directly assume that he is a jerk. To avoid falling into this trap, we should always consider the so-called situational conditions when valuing other people.

Confirmation Bias

Once we have a specific idea about someone, we usually see everything they do through the filter of these preconceptions. For example, if you consider a co-worker to be selfish, you look at the behaviors that confirm it, but not those who deny it.

Although our first impressions are usually quite reliable, they are not infallible, so it is essential to consider our judgments as we continue to relate to that person. The best way to prevent confirmation bias is to seek evidence that challenges your initial assumptions actively. Psychology calls this process "positive DE confirmation of expectations."

The Wavy Effect

The wavy effect is a cognitive bias whereby we make a generalization wrong from a person's single characteristic. The variable that most causes this effect is physical attractiveness; that is, we tend to value those who seem attractive to us more positively. Similarly, we also tend to value better those who resemble us.

An effective way to understand how it works is to identify when it occurs in critical situations. For example, when you hire someone for a job or when you are in a situation that involves many new people. If we pay attention, we will see that, in both cases, we tend to gravitate towards those people with whom we share certain features, whether physical or cultural background.

Let Us Influence the Past

A bad experience with a postal officer can lead us to assess all civil servants negatively. In the same way, knowing a person who reminds us of someone from our past can influence our judgment about that new person. For example, if the most undesirable person in your class at the school was named Alberto, you will have more difficulty positively assessing a person with that name.

One way to avoid this negative influence is to pay attention to our reactions' proportionality and identify when we approach a situation with a negative or defensive attitude.

The Supposed Similarity Bias

Usually, we tend to assume that others think like us and have our same preferences. But obviously, this is a mistake. If you want to skip this type of cognitive prejudice is to create a habit of warning people about diversity in people's preferences and expectations. That is, allow people to let you know that their comfort zone is different from yours.

Secrets of How to Analyze a Person

You surely wanted to be able to read the minds of other people more than once. With the aid of their formed instincts, some are spared, but if you are not so wise, you have only one way out: learn to decode the body's language.

It's no longer a secret that we get 55% of the information with the aid of non-verbal communication. Face expressions, emotions, and actions of the body will strip anyone's disguise and reveal their true thoughts and feelings.

Closing Your Eyes

If a person closes his eyes, talking to you, you must know that he is trying to hide or protect himself from the outside world. That doesn't mean I'm scared of you. Alternatively, the other way around, He wants to take you out of his dream area. You may already have bored it. Open and bam your head! You're done.

Protecting the Mouth by Hand

It's a vivid example from childhood that we all come. Remember, when you didn't want to say anything, you covered your mouth with the palm of your hand. It's the same person. Many fingertips, fist, or palm allow us to express the words. Sometimes with a feigned cough, we mask it.

Biting the Rim of Your Glasses

Does your buddy intentionally bite his glasses rings? Try to encourage and support him. He must surely be concerned about something, and he wants to feel safe at his subconscious level, as in childhood with the mother's breast. By the way, the same applies to a pencil, pad, finger, cigarette, or even chewing gum in hand.

Stroking the Chin

The person is trying to decide this way. Your attention can be focused downwards, sideways, to the left, or any other side at the same time. He doesn't know what he sees at that exact moment because he's immersed in his feelings.

Crossed Arms

One of the most repeated movements. It is not shocking that many people feel very comfortable with this posture, as this gesture helps separate themselves from others. When we're not happy with something, we use it several times. The crossed arms are a clear sign of your interlocutor's negative attitude.

Self-Exposure

This posture is more accessible, right? When a woman wants to like a friend, by revealing her best sides, she starts to reveal herself. She straightens and bends her thighs to show her breasts. The folded arms below are a clear signal of the interlocutor's attention.

Leaning Forward

Normally, he leans forward when a person feels concerned for their interlocutor and needs to contact him or her. The feet that remain in the same place at the same time, but the body moves unconsciously.

Leaning Back

If the individual leans against his seat's back, he clarifies that the conversation is boring. In your interlocutor's company, you can feel uncomfortable.

Handshake "Glove"

It indicates you can trust him if your interlocutor embraces you with both paws.

Squeeze with Palm Up

The palm-up displays sensitivity, protecting the interlocutor's face, but only if achieved at once. If the hands were already holding for a particular moment, and then somebody placed the hand palm up, it may signify a desire to show who is in charge.

Squeeze with a Touch

The person can touch the forearm, elbow, or back of the person he greets with a single hand. This personal space invasion shows the need for contact. And the smaller the body becomes, the more important it is.

Straightening the Bond

It depends on the situation here. If it's a man who does it in a woman's presence, he may very much like it. But this gesture can also mean the person is not feeling comfortable. You may have been lying or just wanting to leave.

Collecting Non-Existent Hair

The gesture of repression is thus called. We use it most of the time to express their overt dissatisfaction. We don't express their opinion freely, in other words, but we certainly disagree with what's going on around them.

Feet on the Table

This expression can mean many things: bad manners, arrogance, the desire to show off as a great boss, or health concern. Nonetheless, psychologists tend to believe that it would be safer to use it at home or in your relatives' company, even if you are very confident in this role.

Riding the Chair

A chair is not a saddle, and the back is not a shield, although it seems to be in some respects. It was also designed for other uses. This way of sitting around is troubling so many people, so we feel a lot of hostility from the "hung" individual at the intuitive level. Powerful men usually use this position.

Eye Contact

The eyes are the soul's mirror as well as a natural interactive device. There we can read all the interlocutor's feelings and emotions. Lovers look at each other's heads, expecting unintentionally to see how they get larger. And this shows a lot as, relative to their normal state, the pupils will increase in size up to four times. By the way, if the person gets mad, their eyes become like accounts because of the pupils' full reduction.

Chapter 30. Speed Reading to Understand People

If you are ready to read other people, then this is the guide for you. Ultimately, being able to read other people is highly essential. If you want to understand what is going on in someone else's mind, you need to tell what is going on with their bodies first. The truth is, people are quite easy to learn to read if you know what you are doing. All you have to do is make sure that you are looking at specific clusters.

Ultimately, we all communicate with people in different ways. We have both verbal and non-verbal signals that we give off at all times. However, the bulk of our communication is non-verbal. We have plenty of body language that we use in different ways to understand what is going on with other people. We look at proximity to each other and general demeanor to figure out what is going on inside one person's mind to get more information from them. When you do this, you learn to recognize how you can interpret what they are about to do, if they are going to do anything at all.

Within this guide, we will take a look at what it will take for you to begin understanding other people at a glance. You will learn how to understand the basic expressions, attraction, closed behavior, assertiveness, and dominance. All of these are important in their ways, serving essential roles that you can utilize. All you have to do is make sure that you know what to look for!

Reading Expressions

Ultimately, we have seven primary expressions—these are known as our universal expressions because you can spot them pretty much in any culture. Every one of us knows what a smile is, and you can recognize it immediately. That is because a smile is an expression that is considered universal. Let's look at the six universal emotions now so that you can better see what to expect with them.

Happiness

Happiness is easy to understand. When you see someone that's happy, you can recognize it by the smile primarily. However, the most obvious sign of happiness is the crinkle in the eyes—this is how you know that the smile and happiness are legitimate.

Sadness

When it comes to sadness, you can identify it by the fact that the entire face melts. You can see that the eyebrows go down. The corners of the mouth do as well, and the inner corners of the brows go up. There may or may not be crying involved as well.

Anger

Anger is defined by three primary characteristics, aside from the demeanor that goes with it. Usually, someone who is angry will have their brows lowered while pressing their lips together firmly. Alternatively, the mouth may be open, bearing teeth and squared.

Fear

Fear is usually shown as brows up high on the face, but still flat, with the eyes widened. The mouth usually opens widely as well.

Surprise

The surprise is similar to fear in people, but the marked difference is that the jaw lowers alongside the mouth's opening, and the eyes are usually opened wider, showing whites on both sides. The brows are also arched instead of just raised.

Disgust

Disgust is noticed primarily by taking a look at how the face comes together. The upper lip goes up, rising slightly. The nose bridge usually wrinkles as well, and the cheeks pinch in and up to try to protect the eyes.

Reading Attraction

When a person is attracted to someone else, they show undeniable body language as well. In particular, you can expect to see all sorts of specific actions. The body does not usually lie, and because of that, you can look directly at the behaviors that someone is doing to figure out if they are attracted to you or not. In particular, you want to look for the following behaviors:

Sustained Eye Contact

You will see that the other person will maintain eye contact more when attracted to you. Additionally, they will usually look away and then glance right back to see if you're still watching them.

Smiling

There is a reason we assume smiling is flirting—it happens often. The flirty, attracted smile usually lasts longer and includes flirty eye contact, and fleeting, but regular.

Self-grooming

Men and women both do this—they brush their hair with their hands, adjust their clothes, and otherwise tamper with their appearance when they are flirting or talking to someone they find attractive. If they do this regularly, they may be attracted to you.

Looking Nervous

Being nervous is a very normal thing when attracted to someone else, and this usually shows itself through fiddling with something repeatedly.

Leaning in

Typically, people will lean toward things that they are attracted to, and people are no exception to that rule. You will also notice that the feet will point at the person that the individual is attracted to.

Licking the lips

This is a common one, but it is subtle and easy to miss. However, you can notice it if you pay close attention. Usually, it is noticeable by a quick part of the lips and a small suck or lick.

Reading Assertiveness

Assertiveness is calm, confident, and in control. Effectively, if someone is assertive, they behave as if they are in control—they take charge, are comfortable with themselves, and won't go out of their way to overstep on other people. They sit back and allow things to play out without letting anyone else dominate them. The most common signs of assertiveness include:

Smooth Body Movements

When you are assertive over something, you don't have jerky movements. They are smooth and in control without much of a problem, even when energized or emotional. The voice sounds smooth as well, and they slowly and steadily look about.

Balanced

The assertive individual is usually upright, relaxed, but also well balanced and comfortable.

Open Body Language

Usually, these people will show that they are open to engagement without threatening or provocative. They do not block off their bodies at all and show open hands as well.

Eye Contact Regularly

Eye contact is usually steady and maintained comfortably without much of a problem.

Smiling

There are plenty of polite smiles and listening well with this body language as well. Usually, you can expect the other person to be quite comfortable, and they will smile efficiently and appropriately.

Firm

While they are firm, they usually have a solid stance without much of a problem. They are not confrontational and typically show that they are willing to listen, but they are also firm. They do not escalate anything and tend to avoid aggression in any form.

Reading Domination

Domination is a little more than assertiveness. Usually, with assertiveness, you see someone that is showing that they are confident without being threatening. However, with dominance, you can expect to see a much more threatening demeanor. A dominating body is going to show signs such as:

Facial Aggressiveness

You will be able to see the aggression in the face—usually in the form of frowning and sneering or even snarling.

Starring

The aggressive individual will usually stare at someone they don't like or may also squint or attempt to avoid looking at someone entirely.

Widebody Stance

They will usually stand out with their shoulders widened and may even hold their arms wide open as well. They may also stand with their hands placed firmly on their hips in a crotch display.

You may notice sudden movements that the aggressor is very rough with his movements, moving about suddenly and even erratically sometimes. It is a good sign that they are not in a perfect spot and may do something else aggressive.

Large Gestures

You may notice that as the individual moves, he will signal with aggressive, almost too big or wide movements that get close to you without ever getting close enough to touch you.

Reading Closed Behavior

Finally, let's go over closed behavior before we continue. Closed behavior shows that the individual is not interested in engaging with the other party at all. When you see closed behavior, you know that the individual will not want to engage with you; you will see that they want to be left alone. You can expect to see symptoms or signs of this sort of behavior, such as:

Crossed Arms

This is perhaps the most telltale sign. When someone feels closed off, they will almost always cross their arms and keep their hands near their bodies. When they speak during this time, they will keep a monotone voice. Think as your sign that you create a barrier between yourself and the other party with your arms. You want to be alone, so you close yourself off entirely.

Crossed Legs

You can also cross off legs as well—when you do this, you see that the knees are across from each other when sitting down, or they can cross the ankles as well. It creates an even more closed off image that shows that you are defensive and unwilling to listen or change your viewpoint on something.

Looking Away

It is also prevalent to see that the closed-off person wants nothing to do with those around them. They don't want to look at the person that is engaging with them.

Leaning Away

You may also see that the closed-off person wants nothing to do with getting close to the individual engaging with them either.

Instead, they will pull away and lean back, trying to put as much distance between them as possible.

Feet Turned Away

Look to the feet when you want to know how engaged someone else is. If you see that the other person is standing away, feet pointing away from you, they are closed off and don't want to engage in the conversation at all.

Chapter 31. Advanced Tips and Tricks to Control People

So you're playing the seduction game and leading someone to get intimidated by you? Again, manipulation is a powerful weapon in your arsenal that can be used negatively or positively to achieve your objectives with the person, even though it may have largely negative connotations. There are plenty of psychological tricks that can be used to get close to a person or lead them to be intimate with you.

Exercise due caution and diligence when it comes to using these techniques because your dignity and reputation are at stake here. Playing with other people's emotions always to have your way will make you come across as distrustful, deceptive, and selfish.

Flattery

Flattery is a brilliant way to break the ice with someone you've just met or lead someone you know for ages to do what you want. Ensure that you disguise flattery (however fake it is) in the garb of genuine and specific compliments.

For example, instead of telling someone how lovely they look in a particular piece of clothing, say something like, "I love how the color of your eyes is beautifully complemented by what you are wearing." It sounds more genuine and invariably draws the person to you.

There is a secret strategy when it comes to resorting to flattery. Identify an area where the person is slightly insecure and needs reassurance. Use specific compliments related to that area to win over the person. For instance, if someone has issues related to speaking confidently in public, tell them that they have a wonderful voice texture or always use the right words while talking. It directly squashes their concerns and insecurities and makes them feel nice about an area they aren't too sure about.

Make Them Indebted to You

It is another slightly insidious strategy that can be used to seduce a person or get them to do what you want. It is a universal strategy that is effective across cultures, classes, and genders. You make the subject feel indebted to you by doing them a series of favors. In their mind, they become obliged to you even though they didn't ask for it.

You create a misbalanced equation where you are the giver, and they are the receiver. To make the equation more balanced, they know they have to pay you back in some form. Take advantage of this titled balance and get them to do what you want by straightforwardly asking them when the time comes. There are high chances the person has already mentally conditioned himself or herself to pay you back. Evil as it sounds, the tactic is used by several people who will fund others' lifestyles to make them feel indebted to the manipulator. The subtext is, "I own you because I pay for everything you use." It may start with small things that the subject voluntarily opts for, which then becomes impossible to get out of.

Use Shame or Guilt

There's no denying that the manipulation seduction game can get sneaky and complicated with blurred right and wrong lines. However, the manipulator widely uses another technique to charm people into going out or sleeping with them. It comprises inducing feelings of guilt or shame on the subject.

If the manipulator's requests are continuously turned down, he or she will make the subject feel guilty or shameful about refusing them. For example, "You know how lonely I am, living all alone away from my family. I've had a very rough and lonely childhood where no one ever loved or cared for me. You are also adding to my feelings of being lonely and uncared for with your cold and disinterested attitude. I know the world is against me, and no one wants me."

Manipulators know how to induce feelings of guilt by pushing the right emotional buttons. You will make more sweeping statements (no one loves me, the world is against me, or I've had a rough childhood) rather than state-specific instances. Manipulators cleverly study what makes the other person feel guilty and target those areas to get what they want.

Another disturbing yet highly successful seduction manipulation technique is to make the other person feel shameful about their past actions repeatedly. Though it may help you get what you want in the short run, it will certainly not set the basis for a healthy, rewarding, and meaningful relationship in the future.

Steer the Conversation

Seducers who've mastered the art of manipulation will almost always hold the remote control of a conversation to lead their subject into doing what they want. For example, if you want to sweet talk with a date, spouse, crush, or friend who is nagging you about something, you steer the course of the conversation by changing the topic to a more favorable one.

"Hey, I just saw a gorgeous blue, low-cut outfit that would look flattering on you at Mary Ann's boutique the other day" or "I saw the most jaw-droppingly beautiful house at Lakeview Lane on my way to work the other day, what do you think about living there together?" It takes the conversation from a rather unpleasant tone into a more welcoming and inviting tone that sets the pace for wooing someone or triggering feelings of intimacy in them.

False Logic

Teens and adolescents mostly use this one, but there's no denying that plenty of adults resort to it too. The logical fallacy or false logic creation technique comprises creating a seemingly false argument and making it sound that it is indeed true. When you tell someone that if a particular thing is true, they will not do something that you deem undesirable.

For example, "if you love me, you will get married to me immediately" or "if you trust me, you won't hesitate to go to bed with me" You are challenging them to prove their feelings and emotions by getting them to do what you want them to.

Make it Appear Normal

So what you as a manipulator are doing here is making the subject feel like what you've asked for or what you want them to do is normal. To do this, you stealthily use numbers, statistics, and research findings for your advantage. You make someone feel like they think differently, while what you are asking for is normal. This way, they are led into believing that something is wrong with their thinking.

For example, "statistics reveal that 75% of people end up sleeping with each other right after the first date." You establish that it's a norm and that most people would do it, and they are crazy or abnormal if they think otherwise.

Silent Treatment

Seduction experts using manipulation know how to use the silent treatment all too well. It works like magic when you're getting someone to obey your wishes. When you remain silent, it impacts the other person by making them feel like they have done something wrong or hurtful.

They become even more eager to make up for it when they realize that you are hurt, angry, or upset with their actions.

The Mirror Effect

As someone who uses the mirror effect manipulation technique for seducing the subject, you attempt to establish a level of trust and emotional comfort by convincing the other person that you are exactly like them. The manipulator pretends to have the same background, values, interests, personality traits as the subject. You may also share fake stories, secrets, or confessions to build a sense of trust, familiarity, and emotional proximity with the other person. You let them know what they want to hear emotionally, and they return the favor with what you do to them, often sexual.

It is the basis of most seduction-manipulation techniques. Manipulate someone's emotions to lead them to think and feel in a particular way, and then get them to bed with you.

Create a Compelling Want

Seduction is all about creating a compelling desire and then presenting yourself as the source for fulfilling it. It is pretty much what every advertiser, salesperson, and internet marketer use.

They create a specific thing in their prospective clients' lives and then present their products or services as the only solution.

Build a strong need for what you have to offer. Make them feel like they need you to fulfill their physical and emotional objectives. Do not be afraid to show them how you can help them or what you can offer them. Strut your strengths and tease until they are convinced that you've got what they need!

Maintain a little distance from the subject to show them what they desire is slightly out of their reach. They will be yearning for you more when they realize that you have everything they want and are yet out of their reach. It makes them strive for your attention even harder!

Chapter 32. The Most Powerful Mind-Power Tool

Humans spend countless hours seeking new ways to work just about anything. Through endless hours of research, they pour over books and journals looking for the message that will tell them the secret to harnessing mind power. Many never realize that the most powerful mind power tool is already on board and just aching to be used. It is the human brain, the mind itself.

Every time a person practices a new habit or thinks a new thought, they make a new pathway in the brain. Every time the habit is used, or the idea is thought, the nerve pathway becomes even stronger. The human brain is wired at birth to be an efficient machine, and it is ready, from birth, to make an ever-increasing amount of nerve pathways and strengthen the pathways used the most.

Sometimes thoughts and habits need to be changed for the improvement of the person. When people decide that they would like to change their lives, there will be a period of adjustment. It is true whether the change is mental, emotional, or physical. During this period of adjustment, there will be some level of discomfort. When a habit or a thought is already formed, it has made its path in the brain. When a stimulus is seen or heard, the message travels along the preset nerve pathway to the brain's spot that controls that thought or habit. To change a thought or a habit, the nerve path must be changed. Until the nerve path is changed, the old nerve path will remain in the brain. The brain's discomfort is trying to access the old pathway, and the new pathway simultaneously automatically. It is painful for the brain to do.

It is easy to become frustrated when the brain goes back to its old thought and habit patterns. Never fall into the habit of placing blame on a lack of willpower. Willpower has nothing to do with it. It is a challenging thing to override preset pathways in the brain. The brain is a very powerful tool. When will power fail, and mistakes happen, always remember to use kindness and compassion to deal with the failure? The brain is very efficient at doing what it does. The only way to change the brain's pathways is to keep working on new pathways that will eventually obliterate the old, undesirable ones.

The brain needs a clear understanding that changes are about to occur, and new pathways are about to be laid down. Remind the brain that new habits and new thoughts will be replacing the old ones. Blaming failure on a lack of willpower is a self-defeating statement. The process of making new nerve paths in the brain takes hard work and time. It will help to keep reminding oneself of the impending change. By doing this over and over, it makes the process no longer about possible character flaws. The focus is now put on the habit of thought that is being built.

Is it possible to build new nerve pathways in the brain? Yes, it is possible, and it can be done. If more proof is needed, compare the adult brain to the baby's brain. Every current habit and thought a person has the direct result of practicing them repeatedly until they created a brain pathway. New pathways can be created. The baby's brain has no idea of anything. It has no thoughts or habits. Every nerve path currently in the brain was practiced until it became a part of the brain. Think of the baby. The baby lies around day after day and does baby things. Then one day, the baby notices the shiny rattle that mommy is waving in front of its little face. The baby wants the rattle. As the baby is waving its tiny arms around, the mommy puts the rattle close enough so the baby can touch it with its wavering hand. After a few of these sessions, the baby gets the idea that it can touch the rattle if the arm is in the air. A nerve pathway is beginning to grow. So the baby decides to lift its arm to reach for the rattle actively. The baby will be unsuccessful because the arms will wave wildly and will not connect with the rattle. One day, the baby will grab the rattle, and the nerve pathway is then complete.

While this may seem like a straightforward example, it is precisely how nerve pathways are created in the brain. Every action, thought, or habit has its nerve pathway. All pathways must be created. No one was born knowing to sit in front of the television and mindlessly eat dip with chips. No one was born lamenting the excess pounds they carry in strange places. No one was born hating their body; all behaviors are learned, good and bad. And the bad ones can be replaced with good ones.

So if the ability to program negative thoughts into the brain exists, then the ability to disrupt those negative thoughts with positive thoughts also exists. The brain can be reprogrammed. It is a powerful tool, and its main function is to turn thoughts into reality. The brain is always working, so why not use the brain's power to benefit rather than harm? Just because a particular habit or thought has been around forever, it does not mean it needs to stay. Use the brain's power to choose new habits and thoughts to focus on and replace the brain's old, negative thought pathways.

The new thought needs to be believable; the new habit needs to be doable. It does not look really good to try to stick to a habit that is impossible to accomplish or to try to believe an unbelievable thought. After years of seeing an obese body's reality, it would be nearly impossible to suddenly believe that the mirror image is that of a skinny person. But the brain will likely accept something that mentions learning to take care of the body or learning to accept the body to correct its flaws. The brain will turn a belief into reality. Believing a positive thought will lead to a different result than the ending where only negative thoughts are present.

Be prepared to repeat and repeat some more. The primary key to being able to make a new habit stay is repeating it constantly. The more a new, desirable habit is practiced, the more the brain begins to accept it. The nerve path becomes stronger every day. With constant practice, this new nerve path will become the path the brain will prefer to use, and the old one will cease to exist.

In any case, be sure to allow enough time to create a change effectively. Accept the starting point and continuously visualize the ending point. Accept that the path to the goal of a new habit or thought will not be easy or perfect. The path will rarely travel in a straight line. Sometimes people fall entirely off the path, and that is okay too. Do not get sidetracked by the idea that this journey will be comfortable and carefree because it will not be. Just keep thinking of the new nerve pathway created by the new thought or habit, and it will eventually become a reality.

Most of the pathways in the brain are stored in the subconscious mind. It is the part of the mind that is always working without always being thought of. Think of learned skills like tying shoes, zipping a coat, and pouring milk into a glass. These were all learned behavior whose nerve pathways are firmly set in the subconscious part of the mind. This part of the brain is the bank of data for all life functions.

The communication between the conscious mind and the unconscious mind works in both directions. Whenever a person has a memory, and emotion, or an idea, it is rooted in the subconscious mind and translated to the conscious mind through mind power. The subconscious has the power to control just about anything a human regularly does.

For example, during meditation, steady, deep breathing is usually practiced. The control of the breath is brought from the subconscious mind and given to the conscious mind to control the breathing. Once a pattern of deep, steady breathing is begun by the conscious mind, the subconscious mind takes over and keeps the set rhythm going until it is told to stop. It is done by a conscious end to deep breathing. The subconscious mind also processes the great wealth of information received daily and only passes along to the conscious mind those necessary for the brain to remember.

When sending thoughts from the conscious mind to the subconscious mind, the brain will only send those thoughts attached to great emotion. The only thoughts that remain in the subconscious are those that are kept there with strong emotions. Unfortunately, the brain does not know the difference between positive emotions and negative emotions. Any strong emotion will work. Both negative emotions and positive emotions can be quite strong. Also, unfortunately, negative emotions tend to be stronger than positive emotions.

Step one in learning to use the subconscious part of the mind's power will be to eliminate any thoughts that come with negative emotions. Also, negative mental comments will need to cease. Fears will usually come true, precisely because they are drowning in negative emotion. Negative ideas need to be eliminated because they can be very harmful roadblocks on the road to harnessing brainpower.

One best practice to use to get rid of negative thoughts is to counter them with positive thoughts. It will take time and practice, but it is a very powerful and useful technique. Whenever a negative thought pops in the conscious mind, immediately counter it with a positive thought dripping with strong emotion. The actual truth will come out somewhere in between the two thoughts.

Another way to counter negative emotions is to delete them, just like using a remote control. When a negative thought comes into the conscious mind, imagine destroying it. Imagine writing that thought on paper and burning it. Imagine pointing a remote control at the thought and pressing a huge delete button. Whatever form used to imagine deleting the thought, the important thing is to get rid of it before taking hold in the subconscious mind.

Find something energizing and use it to reach a goal. Those things that are found to be energizing bring boundless energy to positive thoughts. It is often necessary to invent motivation to learn to create new habits and thoughts, at least in the beginning. But with a bit of practice and a lot of positive thought, new positive habits will soon be burned into the subconscious mind, and the old negative thoughts and habits will fade away.

Conclusion

You learned all about NLP, persuasion, and other subjects connected to these two. Remember all of the body languages you were taught—out of everything, that maybe one of the best skills to foster and develop. You learned of several different ways people can control, influence, and persuade other people to do what they want or need. You learned all about how people prefer to interact with others and genuinely and naturally develop the persuasion and influence that so many people desire. You were also taught how to develop several social skills that are of the utmost importance if you wish to be successful.

Ultimately, the information should guide your behaviors. Let this allow you to go through your life, be informed, and aware of how your behaviors influence others. Focus on those around you with their body language and see how easily your behaviors can sway them. Learn from negotiation skills to ensure that you can get what you want while still giving back to others. Remember how to keep your interactions with those around you ethical, even if you understand how to take over and manipulate them into obedience to do whatever it is you are seeking.

Neuro-linguistic Programming practitioners and trainers have put forward exemplary approaches and techniques to persuade, which can be used in various environments. Studies state that these techniques develop personal performances and help the individual maintain good intrapersonal and interpersonal relationships.

To persuade someone entails a process of altering and rebuilding their opinions, beliefs, values, and behaviors towards an outcome. Humans are programmed to find it extremely difficult to move out of their comfort zone, no matter their comfort zone. For some individuals, even if their comfort is unhealthy, they wouldn't mind staying in it because, well, it's comfortable.

Persuasion is just not about forcing an individual to behave how we want them to behave; it is about allowing them to come out of their comfort zone to achieve a higher comfort zone after the discomfort of the change subsides. Simply put, an individual who regularly smokes will keep smoking because it is his comfort zone. To persuade or convince him will be a pretty challenging task because quitting is uncomfortable for the person. During the non-smoking period, this person might go through considerable discomfort. Still, afterward, he will experience a higher comfort zone due to the absence of his unhealthy behavior.

For persuasion to be successful, the person tries to persuade the individual to figure out what is essential to the individual. The persuader should identify factors that can eventually give the individual a higher level of comfort. For a person who finds staying at home and shunning social life comforting, the persuader should discover a factor that can allow them to move outside the box. By helping them realize that although going out can be, they will have a higher sense of comfort once they achieve their goals. This process needs a skilled persuader to assure the client that the behavior change will make them feel more comfortable.

Advantages of NLP

These NLP techniques can increase the level of influence that you exert on others. Companies that engage in marketing and sales depend entirely on persuading their clients or clients to buy their products; the strategies presented in NLP guide these sellers and dealers to increase the chance of influencing their clients in making decisions. NLP also increases the person's performance; NLP helps you modify and replace your negative behaviors with more positive ones. These strategies also help you to improve your leadership style. Being humble and non-judgmental allows you to have a better communication style, even outside the persuasion process.

Essentials for Persuasion

Empathy

This is an essential quality that a persuader requires. You should not only be thinking about yourself, but you also should try to put yourself in the other person's shoes and think about how they might be feeling. Empathy also helps deter you from being judgmental.

Listening Skills

Only a good listener will persuade another person; a person who is always ready for an argument will never be a good listener. If you want to be a good and positive persuader, you need to listen to what the other individual says and pay attention to their body language.

Indirect and Clever Commands

People tend to be more responsive to suggestions than questions. For example, instead of using the words "Would you like to go to the concert?" You can say "Come, let's go to the concert"; this motivates a more positive response from the individual.

Restrict the Choices That You Provide

Try not to allow the individual to say "No." Taking the same example, instead of asking, "Will you be able to stay long at the concert?" ask them, "Would you like to stay here for three hours or four?" The latter question makes it hard for the individual to say a "No."

Allow the Person to Visualize

Successful persuaders always help the client, or the individual visualize to convince them. An example would be, "this concert will make us scream the lyrics of our favorite songs."

Always Make It Simple as Possible

Trying to convince the other person by bragging will only be a failure; keep it as simple as possible and remember you should never put their views down.

You can use the information you were provided for good. You can use it to better your relationships, your career, and your social life. If you understand how people interact with others, you can ensure that you are interacting positively. You can make every interaction with other people positive and fulfilling for everyone involved. Above all, you can naturally develop the skills you need to create and earn your leadership skills. People will naturally seek to follow you if you build your NLP and persuasion techniques. People will listen to you better if you have advanced social skills. You can use it to your advantage to ensure that you and those around you are happy with life. Use your enlightenment and knowledge for good, and go out there, armed with the knowledge you need to persuade others, both for your benefit and theirs.

So, what are you still waiting for? It is time to embrace this guide so that you'll allow the light inside you to radiate without fear of hurting others of being all that you are meant to be. This guide will help you overcome manipulation so that you can shine brighter!

www.ingramcontent.com/pod-product-compliance
Lightning Source LLC
Chambersburg PA
CBHW060334030426
42336CB00011B/1336